Come to Jesus

Written by Christopher Newman Hall

Compiled, updated, edited and ESV® Scripture added

by

Chuck Cibes

Table of Contents

Preface

This book, which was originally called a tract, was written by an Englishman, Christopher Newman Hall. He was acquainted with Charles Spurgeon and on occasion would preach from Spurgeon's pulpit. This was written in 1848 and was published circa 1863 by the Evangelical Tract Society in Petersburg, VA which at that time was part of the Confederate States of America.

According to Chaplain J. William Jones in his book *Christ in the Camp*, this tract was in great demand in the Confederate Army during the War Between the States, was very well received, and many men came to Jesus through reading this tract and the referenced Scriptures.

I have updated some of the language to more modern terms, and have included the actual Scripture that Hall referenced. It's been my experience that few people actually take the time and effort to look up and read the referenced verses. Knowing that the Holy Spirit works more through God's Word than through man's words, I wanted to make those verses readily available.

I would suggest reading a chapter a day for a month, since there are 31 chapters.

It is my hope and prayer that many will read this book and Come to Jesus, just as they did 150 years ago; come to a saving knowledge of Christ.

--Chuck Cibes, near Tigerville, SC

Chapter One

COME TO JESUS

LISTEN, dear fellow-sinner. How kind, how wonderful an invitation is this! God speaks, and speaks to YOU. The Father says, "COME." The Son says, "COME." The Holy Spirit says, "COME." The blessed angels echo the cry, "COME." Many poor sinners who have accepted the call, join their voices in the appeal, and say to you, "Come to Jesus." This little book unites in the entreaty, poor sinner, and with all earnestness, plainness and affection, implores you to "COME to JESUS."

When he was himself on earth, well knowing and full of pity for the sufferings and sins of men, as he looked around on the crowd which one day surrounded him, he tenderly said, "Come to me, all who labor and are heavy laden, and I will give you rest. Take my yoke upon you, and learn from me, for I am gentle and lowly in heart, and you will find rest for your souls. For my yoke is easy, and my burden is light." What he said then he says NOW. The invitation he gave to the men of that day, he gives to you, my fellow-sinner: "Come unto me.', Are you not loaded down with guilt? O then come to Jesus and you shall find rest. COME TO JESUS; COME TO JESUS.

COME TO JESUS.

He promises rest. But far better than rest of body is rest of soul. It is wretched to be a slave, to groan, bleed, toil; but far worse to be Satan's bondman, dragging about an evil conscience and an aching heart. Rest from this cannot be had except by coming to Jesus. And if we come, he will lighten every other load. Are you poor? Come, and he will make you rich for ever. Probably not in the material things of this earth, which will all burn sooner or later anyway, but certainly in spiritual ways. Lay up your treasure in heaven where it will never rust or decay or mysteriously disappear -and will be there forever. Are you sad? Come, and he will be a comfort as he walks beside you. Are you bereaved? Come, and he will be to you a brother in adversity, who never changes, and never dies. Is sin a burden? O then come to Jesus and he will take it all away. Do you dread the day of death and judgment? Come, and that day will be the dawn of life and glory. O then come.

To be merely called by such a person should be enough to make us glad. If a stranger called, we might say, "Perhaps he intends me no good;" if a poor man called, "He cannot assist me, however willing;" if a selfish rich man, "Who can expect anything from him?" But if a man such as a Spurgeon or a Wilberforce said to a mourner, "Come," he might feel quite sure some kindness was intended. Now he who invites you, sinner, is both able and willing to help. He has the most important gift possible, spiritual peace and eternal life for all. His very word, "Come," is enough to make you glad.

A blind beggar by the wayside, hearing he was passing, cried out, "Mercy, mercy!" The people told him to be quiet; but he shouted all the louder, "Have mercy on me!" Jesus invited him: and then some said, knowing that he might now be quite sure of a blessing, "Be of good comfort; rise, he calls you." They knew Jesus never called and then refused; and so they told him to rejoice. Sinner, you can be of good cheer; this same Jesus calls you. As the blind man threw off his cloak in case it should hinder him, you must cast off every sin that would stop you--rush through every crowd of difficulties, and falling at the feet of Jesus say, "Have mercy on me? I am blind, I am lost; save me, or I will perish." Do you think that you are too great a sinner? The more you need to come. Do you have a guilty conscience? With that guilty conscience come. Do you have a wicked heart? With that wicked heart come. Do you have nothing with which to purchase his favor? "Without money" come, his gift is free. Rich and poor, masters and servants, old and young, white man and black, sinners, of every class, COME.

Isaiah 55:1-13 "Come, everyone who thirsts, come to the waters; and he who has no money, come, buy and eat! Come, buy wine and milk without money and without price. Why do you spend your money for that which is not bread, and your labor for that which does not satisfy? Listen diligently to me, and eat what is good, and delight yourselves in rich food. Incline your ear, and come to me; hear, that your soul may live; and I will make with you an everlasting covenant, my steadfast, sure love for David. Behold, I made him a witness to the peoples, a leader and commander for the peoples. Behold, you shall call a nation that you do not know, and a nation that did not know you

3

shall run to you, because of the LORD your God, and of the Holy One of Israel, for he has glorified you.

"Seek the LORD while he may be found; call upon him while he is near; let the wicked forsake his way, and the unrighteous man his thoughts; let him return to the LORD, that he may have compassion on him, and to our God, for he will abundantly pardon. For my thoughts are not your thoughts, neither are your ways my ways, declares the LORD. For as the heavens are higher than the earth, so are my ways higher than your ways and my thoughts than your thoughts. "For as the rain and the snow come down from heaven and do not return there but water the earth, making it bring forth and sprout, giving seed to the sower and bread to the eater, so shall my word be that goes out from my mouth; it shall not return to me empty, but it shall accomplish that which I purpose, and shall succeed in the thing for which I sent it. "For you shall go out in joy and be led forth in peace; the mountains and the hills before you shall break forth into singing, and all the trees of the field shall clap their hands. Instead of the thorn shall come up the cypress; instead of the brier shall come up the myrtle; and it shall make a name for the LORD, an everlasting sign that shall not be cut off."

Matthew 8:1-17 When he came down from the mountain, great crowds followed him. And behold, a leper came to him and knelt before him, saying, "Lord, if you will, you can make me clean." And Jesus stretched out his hand and touched him, saying, "I will; be clean." And immediately his leprosy was cleansed. And Jesus said to him, "See that you say nothing to anyone, but go, show yourself to the priest and offer the gift that Moses commanded, for a proof to them."

When he had entered Capernaum, a centurion came forward to him, appealing to him, "Lord, my servant is lying paralyzed at home, suffering terribly." And he said to him, "I will come and heal him." But the centurion replied, "Lord, I am not worthy to have you come under my roof, but only say the word, and my servant will be healed. For I too am a man under authority, with soldiers under me. And I say to one, 'Go,' and he goes, and to another, 'Come,' and he comes, and to my servant, 'Do this,' and he does it." When Jesus heard this, he marveled and said to those who followed him, "Truly, I tell you, with no one in Israel have I found such faith.

I tell you, many will come from east and west and recline at table with Abraham, Isaac, and Jacob in the kingdom of heaven, while the sons of the kingdom will be thrown into the outer darkness. In that place there will be weeping and gnashing of teeth."

And to the centurion Jesus said, "Go; let it be done for you as you have believed." And the servant was healed at that very moment.

And when Jesus entered Peter's house, he saw his mother-in-law lying sick with a fever. He touched her hand, and the fever left her, and she rose and began to serve him.

That evening they brought to him many who were oppressed by demons, and he cast out the spirits with a word and healed all who were sick. This was to fulfill what was spoken by the prophet Isaiah: "He took our illnesses and bore our diseases."

Matthew 11:28-30 Come to me, all who labor and are heavy laden, and I will give you rest. Take my yoke upon you, and learn from me, for I am gentle and lowly in heart, and you will find rest for your souls. For my yoke is easy, and my burden is light."

Mark 10:46-52 And they came to Jericho. And as he was leaving Jericho with his disciples and a great crowd, Bartimaeus, a blind beggar, the son of Timaeus, was sitting by the roadside. And when he heard that it was Jesus of Nazareth, he began to cry out and say, "Jesus, Son of David, have mercy on me!" And many rebuked him, telling him to be silent. But he cried out all the more, "Son of David, have mercy on me!" And Jesus stopped and said, "Call him." And they called the blind man, saying to him, "Take heart. Get up; he is calling you." And throwing off his cloak, he sprang up and came to Jesus. And Jesus said to him, "What do you want me to do for you?" And the blind man said to him, "Rabbi, let me recover my sight." And Jesus said to him, "Go your way; your faith has made you well." And immediately he recovered his sight and followed him on the way.

Revelation 22:17 The Spirit and the Bride say, "Come." And let the one who hears say, "Come." And let the one who is thirsty come; let the one who desires take the water of life without price.

Chapter 2

WHY SHOULD I COME?

YOU ARE A SINNER, COME FOR PARDON

Perhaps you do not feel you are a sinner. At least, you think you are no worse than others, but better than many. You are no drunkard, thief, adulterer, but keep the Sabbath, read the Bible, and attend the house of God. But have you indeed obeyed all the commandments? Never broken a single one? Always been true, chaste, sober, honest, forgiving, kind? Never indulged in pride, malice, anger, deceit, or lust?

God requires purity of heart as well as of outward conduct, and he knows all our thoughts. Have you then never cherished the thought of sin in your heart, though you have feared outwardly to commit it? Besides, the first and chief command is, to love the Lord our God with all our mind and strength. Have you always done this; always been thankful for his mercies; always carefully read his word in order to obey it; always tried to please him, loved to pray to him, taken delight in his day, his people, his worship; always striven to be "holy as he is holy," to make known his truth, to induce others to love him, and endeavored in all things to glorify him? If you have always done this, you have still only just done your duty, and have nothing to boast of. But you have not done it. Conscience tells you so.

You know you have sinned thousands of times. You know you have sought your own pleasure, and in your best actions you have not been prompted by a desire to please God. You have lived for yourself; you have sought man's approval, but God has not been in all your thoughts. The Bible tells us, "If man says he has no sin, he deceives himself. There is none righteous, no, not one. All have sinned, and come short of the glory of God." O, my fellow-sinner, is it not true of you, "The God in whose hand is your breath, and whose are all your ways, you have not honored?"

You are a sinner. Guilt, enormous guilt hangs upon you. In God's book all your sins are written down. You cannot get rid of them. Were you to labor for thousands of years, you could not atone for the least. All you could do would only be your duty. Paying today's debt still leaves yesterday's where it was. And were you to give all you possess, or suffer torture and death, it would not take away sin. The past cannot be recalled. But there is forgiveness, free, full, eternal, for the guilty. Jesus has pardon for you, sinner, purchased with his own blood. Come for it. Come to Jesus Christ for it.

Exodus 20:1-18 And God spoke all these words, saying, "I am the LORD your God, who brought you out of the land of Egypt, out of the house of slavery.

"You shall have no other gods before me.

"You shall not make for yourself a carved image, or any likeness of anything that is in heaven above, or that is in the earth beneath, or that is in the water under the earth.

"You shall not bow down to them or serve them, for I the LORD your God am a jealous God, visiting the iniquity of the fathers on the children to the third and the fourth generation of those who hate me, but showing steadfast love to thousands of those who love me and keep my commandments.

"You shall not take the name of the LORD your God in vain, for the LORD will not hold him guiltless who takes his name in vain.

"Remember the Sabbath day, to keep it holy. Six days you shall labor, and do all your work, but the seventh day is a Sabbath to the LORD your God. On it you shall not do any work, you, or your son, or your daughter, your male servant, or your female servant, or your livestock, or the sojourner who is within your gates. For in six days the LORD made heaven and earth, the sea, and all that is in them, and rested on the seventh day. Therefore the LORD blessed the Sabbath day and made it holy.

"Honor your father and your mother, that your days may be long in the land that the LORD your God is giving you.

"You shall not murder.

"You shall not commit adultery.

"You shall not steal. "You shall not bear false witness against your neighbor.

"You shall not covet your neighbor's house; you shall not covet your neighbor's wife, or his male servant, or his female servant, or his ox, or his donkey, or anything that is your neighbor's."

Now when all the people saw the thunder and the flashes of lightning and the sound of the trumpet and the mountain smoking, the people were afraid and trembled, and they stood far off

Psalm 51:3-13 For I know my transgressions, and my sin is ever before me. Against you, you only, have I sinned and done what is evil in your sight, so that you may be justified in your words and blameless in your judgment.

Behold, I was brought forth in iniquity, and in sin did my mother conceive me. Behold, you delight in truth in the inward being, and you teach me wisdom in the secret heart. Purge me with hyssop, and I shall be clean; wash me, and I shall be whiter than snow. Let me hear joy and gladness; let the bones that you have broken rejoice. Hide your face from my sins, and blot out all my iniquities.

Create in me a clean heart, O God, and renew a right spirit within me. Cast me not away from your presence, and take not your Holy Spirit from me. Restore to me the joy of your salvation, and uphold me with a willing spirit.

Then I will teach transgressors your ways, and sinners will return to you.

Matthew 5:1-48 Seeing the crowds, he went up on the mountain, and when he sat down, his disciples came to him. And he opened his mouth and taught them, saying:

"Blessed are the poor in spirit, for theirs is the kingdom of heaven.

"Blessed are those who mourn, for they shall be comforted.

"Blessed are the meek, for they shall inherit the earth. Blessed are those who hunger and thirst for righteousness, for they shall be satisfied.

"Blessed are the merciful, for they shall receive mercy.

"Blessed are the pure in heart, for they shall see God.

"Blessed are the peacemakers, for they shall be called sons of God.

"Blessed are those who are persecuted for righteousness' sake, for theirs is the kingdom of heaven.

"Blessed are you when others revile you and persecute you and utter all kinds of evil against you falsely on my account. Rejoice and be glad, for your reward is great in heaven, for so they persecuted the prophets who were before you.

"You are the salt of the earth, but if salt has lost its taste, how shall its saltiness be restored? It is no longer good for anything except to be thrown out and trampled under people's feet.

"You are the light of the world. A city set on a hill cannot be hidden. Nor do people light a lamp and put it under a basket, but on a stand, and it gives light to all in the house. In the same way, let your light shine before others, so that they may see your good works and give glory to your Father who is in heaven.

"Do not think that I have come to abolish the Law or the Prophets; I have not come to abolish them but to fulfill them. For truly, I say to you, until heaven and earth pass away, not an iota, not a dot, will pass from the Law until all is accomplished. Therefore whoever relaxes one of the least of these commandments and teaches others to do the same will be called least in the kingdom of heaven, but whoever does them and teaches them will be called great in the kingdom of heaven. For I tell you, unless your righteousness exceeds that of the scribes and Pharisees, you will never enter the kingdom of heaven.

"You have heard that it was said to those of old, 'You shall not murder; and whoever murders will be liable to judgment.' But I say to you that everyone who is angry with his brother will be liable to judgment; whoever insults his brother will be liable to the council; and whoever says, 'You fool!' will be liable to the hell of fire. So if you are offering your gift at the altar and there remember that your brother has something against you, leave your gift there before the altar and go. First be reconciled to your brother, and then come and offer your gift.

"Come to terms quickly with your accuser while you are going with him to court, lest your accuser hand you over to the judge, and the judge to the guard, and you be put in prison. Truly, I say to you, you will never get out until you have paid the last penny.

"You have heard that it was said, 'You shall not commit adultery.' But I say to you that everyone who looks at a woman with lustful intent has already committed adultery with her in his heart. If your right eye causes you to sin, tear it out and throw it away. For it is better that you lose one of your members than that your whole body be thrown into hell. And if your right hand causes you to sin, cut it off and throw it away. For it is better that you lose one of your members than that your whole body go into hell.

"It was also said, 'Whoever divorces his wife, let him give her a certificate of divorce.' But I say to you that everyone who divorces his wife, except on the ground of sexual immorality, makes her commit adultery, and whoever marries a divorced woman commits adultery.

"Again you have heard that it was said to those of old, 'You shall not swear falsely, but shall perform to the Lord what you have sworn.' But I say to you, Do not take an oath at all, either by heaven, for it is the throne of God, or by the earth, for it is his footstool, or by Jerusalem, for it is the city of the great King. And do not take an oath by your head, for you cannot make one hair white or black. Let what you say be simply 'Yes' or 'No'; anything more than this comes from evil.

"You have heard that it was said, 'An eye for an eye and a tooth for a tooth.' But I say to you, Do not resist the one who is evil. But if anyone slaps you on the right cheek, turn to him the other also. And if anyone would sue you and take your tunic, let him have your cloak as well. And if anyone forces you to go one mile, go with him two miles. Give to the one who begs from you, and do not refuse the one who would borrow from you.

"You have heard that it was said, 'You shall love your neighbor and hate your enemy.' But I say to you, Love your enemies and pray for those who persecute you, so that you may be sons of your Father who is in heaven. For he makes his sun rise on the evil and on the good, and sends rain on the just and on the unjust. For if you love those who love you, what reward do you have? Do not even the tax collectors do the same? And if you greet only your brothers, what more are you doing than others? Do not even the Gentiles do the same? You therefore must be perfect, as your heavenly Father is perfect."

Romans 3:10-20 as it is written: "None is righteous, no, not one; no one understands; no one seeks for God. All have turned aside; together they have become worthless; no one does good, not even one."

"Their throat is an open grave; they use their tongues to deceive." "The venom of asps is under their lips." "Their mouth is full of curses and bitterness."

"Their feet are swift to shed blood; in their paths are ruin and misery, and the way of peace they have not known." "There is no fear of God before their eyes."

Now we know that whatever the law says it speaks to those who are under the law, so that every mouth may be stopped, and the whole world may be held accountable to God. For by works of the law no human being will be justified in his sight, since through the law comes knowledge of sin.

Romans 3:23 for all have sinned and fall short of the glory of God,

1 John 1:8-10 If we say we have no sin, we deceive ourselves, and the truth is not in us. If we confess our sins, he is faithful and just to forgive us our sins and to cleanse us from all unrighteousness. If we say we have not sinned, we make him a liar, and his word is not in us.

Chapter 3

GOD IS ANGRY--COME TO BE RECONCILED

The Bible says "God is angry with the wicked every day". "He hates all who do wrong." And doesn't God have much cause to be angry with you, sinner? He gave and preserves your life and faculties, and bestows all your comforts. Yet you forget him. He has told you his commands; and these are all intended to do you good, yet you do not regard them. You do not reverence God, but live almost as if there was no such Being.

What an ungrateful son would you be, if you treated your parents this way--if you avoided their company, disliked thinking of them, and disregarded their wishes! Hear then what God says: "Hear, O heavens, and be astonished, O earth! I have nourished and brought up children, and they have rebelled against me." He is full of love to you, as a tender Father; but by your sins you have grieved him. Besides, he is your Creator, King, and righteous Judge, and must and will punish all sinners. He must act, to those who rebel, not as a kind parent, but as an angry monarch.

It is your own fault, however, that he is angry. You make him that way. Your sins separate you and God. As long as you live without repenting of sin, his anger must always be hot against you, sinner, and you cannot escape or hide from him. Wherever you are, he is there, and he is angry. He searches out your path and your lying down and he is angry. It depends on him whether or not you draw your very next breath, and he is angry.

O sinner, better for all the world to be angry with you than God to be angry with you. What an awful life is yours! The "wrath of God abides on you." How dreadful to feel when going to bed, "God is angry"--to wake and know "God is angry,"--wherever you go, and whatever you do, "God is angry." And O, to die knowing that "God is angry;" and to stand before his judgment seat, and see that he is angry.

Sinner, he is angry only while you make him so; he is willing to be your friend; he sent his Son with this message, "Be reconciled to God." If you will give your heart to that Messenger, and trust in him, all this anger will cease. O then, come to Jesus. Do not be God's foe any longer, but accept the offer to be his friend. But beware, beware of rejecting Jesus; for he says, "He that believes not," that is, does not come to "the Son, shall not see life, but the wrath of God abides on him."

John 3:36 Whoever believes in the Son has eternal life; whoever does not obey the Son shall not see life, but the wrath of God remains on him.

Psalm 7:11 God is a righteous judge, and a God who feels indignation every day.

Psalm 11:5-6 The LORD tests the righteous, but his soul hates the wicked and the one who loves violence. Let him rain coals on the wicked; fire and sulfur and a scorching wind shall be the portion of their cup.

Psalm 21:8-9 Your hand will find out all your enemies; your right hand will find out those who hate you. You will make them as a blazing oven when you appear. The LORD will swallow them up in his wrath, and fire will consume them.

Romans 1:18 For the wrath of God is revealed from heaven against all ungodliness and unrighteousness of men, who by their unrighteousness suppress the truth.

Romans 2:5-9 But because of your hard and impenitent heart you are storing up wrath for yourself on the day of wrath when God's righteous judgment will be revealed. He will render to each one according to his works: to those who by patience in well-doing seek for glory and honor and immortality, he will give eternal life; but for those who are self-seeking and do not obey the truth, but obey unrighteousness, there will be wrath and fury. There will be tribulation and distress for every human being who does evil, the Jew first and also the Greek,

2 Corinthians 5:18-21 All this is from God, who through Christ reconciled us to himself and gave us the ministry of reconciliation; that is, in Christ God was reconciling the world to himself, not counting their trespasses against them, and entrusting to us the message of

reconciliation. Therefore, we are ambassadors for Christ, God making his appeal through us. We implore you on behalf of Christ, be reconciled to God. For our sake he made him to be sin who knew no sin, so that in him we might become the righteousness of God.

Ephesians 5:6 Let no one deceive you with empty words, for because of these things the wrath of God comes upon the sons of disobedience.

2 Thessalonians 1:7-9 and to grant relief to you who are afflicted as well as to us, when the Lord Jesus is revealed from heaven with his mighty angels in flaming fire, inflicting vengeance on those who do not know God and on those who do not obey the gospel of our Lord Jesus. They will suffer the punishment of eternal destruction, away from the presence of the Lord and from the glory of his might,

Chapter 4

HELL AWAITS YOU--COME TO BE SAVED

Hell is not a fable invented by priests to frighten their fellow-men; but as sure as the Bible is the word of God, so sure is it that "the wicked shall go down into hell, and all nations that forget God." "it is appointed for man to die once, and after that comes judgment." "Then all men must give an account of the deeds done in the body." "God will judge the secrets of men." Then all sinners who have not obtained pardon by coming to Jesus will be on the left hand of the Judge, who will pronounce their dreadful sentence, "Depart from me, you cursed, into the eternal fire prepared for the devil and his angels."

O who can tell the torments of that place? No more pleasant light of day, no more cheerful voice of friends, no more comforts of home, no more pleasures of the world and sin. The rich man can take none of his wealth with him, the carefree man none of his amusements. Past sins will be clearly remembered, and past opportunities of escape now gone for ever. O, for just one more opportunity!! O for one more Sabbath! O for one more hour to pray for mercy! But it will be then too late, too late. Darkness for ever, sin for ever, woe for ever, death for ever. Jesus speaks of it as "the lake that burns with fire and brimstone --outer darkness, where there is weeping and wailing and gnashing of teeth-- where the worm does not die, and the fire is not quenched"--where the wicked rich man, being in torment, cried out, "Send Lazarus, that he may dip the tip of his finger in water, and cool my tongue, for I am tormented in this flame." There he that is filthy shall be "filthy still," and "the smoke of their torment ascends up for ever and ever."

What misery can be greater than what such words as these describe? How dreadful, then, to be in hell! What can be more horrible? And every unforgiven sinner is on his way to it. You whose eye now reads this page, if you are not pardoned, you are on your way. Every hour brings you nearer. Once there, and all hope is gone for ever. But is there no escape? Yes; one way, and one way only. Flee to Jesus. He came to save from hell. "God so loved the world that he gave his only son that whoever believes in him, should not perish, but have everlasting life."

Nothing can save you if you will not come; nothing can prevent your salvation, if you do come.

Matthew 18:1-13 At that time the disciples came to Jesus, saying, "Who is the greatest in the kingdom of heaven?" And calling to him a child, he put him in the midst of them and said, "Truly, I say to you, unless you turn and become like children, you will never enter the kingdom of heaven. Whoever humbles himself like this child is the greatest in the kingdom of heaven. Whoever receives one such child in my name receives me, but whoever causes one of these little ones who believe in me to sin, it would be better for him to have a great millstone fastened around his neck and to be drowned in the depth of the sea. Woe to the world for temptations to sin! For it is necessary that temptations come, but woe to the one by whom the temptation comes!

"And if your hand or your foot causes you to sin, cut it off and throw it away. It is better for you to enter life crippled or lame than with two hands or two feet to be thrown into the eternal fire. And if your eye causes you to sin, tear it out and throw it away. It is better for you to enter life with one eye than with two eyes to be thrown into the hell of fire.

"See that you do not despise one of these little ones. For I tell you that in heaven their angels always see the face of my Father who is in heaven.

"What do you think? If a man has a hundred sheep, and one of them has gone astray, does he not leave the ninety-nine on the mountains and go in search of the one that went astray? And if he finds it, truly, I say to you, he rejoices over it more than over the ninety-nine that never went astray.'"

Luke 16:19-31 "There was a rich man who was clothed in purple and fine linen and who feasted sumptuously every day. And at his gate was laid a poor man named Lazarus, covered with sores, who desired to be fed with what fell from the rich man's table. Moreover, even the dogs came and licked his sores. The poor man died and was carried by the angels to Abraham's side. The rich man also died and was buried, and in Hades, being in torment, he lifted up his eyes and saw Abraham far off and Lazarus at his side. And he called out, 'Father Abraham, have mercy on me, and send Lazarus to dip the end of his finger in water and cool my tongue, for I am in anguish in this flame.' But Abraham said, 'Child, remember that you in your lifetime received your good things, and Lazarus in like manner bad things; but now he is comforted here, and you are in anguish. And besides all this, between us and you a great chasm has been fixed, in order that those who would pass from here to you may not be able, and none may cross from there to us.' And he said, 'Then I beg you, father, to send him to my father's house—for I have five brothers—so that he may warn them, lest they also come into this place of torment.' But Abraham said, 'They have Moses and the Prophets; let them hear them.' And he said, 'No, father Abraham, but if someone goes to them from the dead, they will repent.' He said to him, 'If they do not hear Moses and the Prophets, neither will they be convinced if someone should rise from the dead."

Revelation 14:10-11 he also will drink the wine of God's wrath, poured full strength into the cup of his anger, and he will be tormented with fire and sulfur in the presence of the holy angels and in the presence of the Lamb. And the smoke of their torment goes up forever and ever, and they have no rest, day or night,"

Revelation 20:11-15 Then I saw a great white throne and him who was seated on it. From his presence earth and sky fled away, and no place was found for them. And I saw the dead, great and small, standing before the throne, and books were opened. Then another book was opened, which is the book of life. And the dead were judged by

22

what was written in the books, according to what they had done. And the sea gave up the dead who were in it, Death and Hades gave up the dead who were in them, and they were judged, each one of them, according to what they had done. Then Death and Hades were thrown into the lake of fire. This is the second death, the lake of fire. And if anyone's name was not found written in the book of life, he was thrown into the lake of fire.

Revelation 22:11-15 Let the evildoer still do evil, and the filthy still be filthy, and the righteous still do right, and the holy still be holy."

"Behold, I am coming soon, bringing my recompense with me, to repay each one for what he has done. I am the Alpha and the Omega, the first and the last, the beginning and the end."

Blessed are those who wash their robes, so that they may have the right to the tree of life and that they may enter the city by the gates. Outside are the dogs and sorcerers and the sexually immoral and murderers and idolaters, and everyone who loves and practices falsehood.

Chapter 5

FOR PEACE OF CONSCIENCE, COME

"There is no peace", says my God, "to the wicked." Some sinners seem to be at peace, but it is only by refusing to think. They will not consider. But such thoughtlessness is not worthy to be called peace. It is like a man in a sinking ship, who will not examine what is the danger; or like a tradesman, who fancies all is not going well, but will not look into his accounts, lest his mind should be disturbed. So the sinner fancies something is wrong, and afraid of being unhappy, he banishes reflection about God and his soul. Yet every sinner thinks sometimes, and then he must be wretched. When death visits a neighbors house, or enters his own, or threatens himself, and at many other times, the thought will come, "God is angry; my soul is in danger; I am not ready to die." And how such a thought must dampen his pleasure, and disturb his rest.

No, you cannot be at peace till you have obtained pardon. You may try all the pleasures of the world in turn, you may seek to drown thought by plunging deeper and deeper into sin, but you cannot be happy. But when we come to Jesus, all our sins are at once forgiven. We still think of them with sorrow, but we need no more think of them with terror. God says to us, "Your sins and your iniquities will I remember no more." He blots out "all trespasses." He "casts them behind his back into the depths of the sea." They will not be mentioned at the judgment day. "He will abundantly pardon."

He now regards us with love. We need not be afraid of him. He invites us to trust him as a kind friend. Instead of hiding **from** him, as Adam did, we may hide **in** him, as David did, saying, "You are my hiding place." O what a happy change! I am a sinner still, but a sinner pardoned, reconciled, saved. And whatever dreadful things conscience may tell me, Jesus says, "Your sins are forgiven you; go in peace." "Peace I leave with you, my peace I give to you." "Being justified by faith, we have peace with God through our Lord Jesus Christ."

Poor sinner, you and peace have long been strangers. Worldly pleasure is not peace; and nothing can give it while you and God are enemies, and your sins hang heavily on your soul. C o m e t h e n t o Jesus. He both makes and gives peace. Seek pardon through him, and you will soon know what is meant by "the peace of God which passes all understanding."

Isaiah 55:7 let the wicked forsake his way, and the unrighteous man his thoughts; let him return to the LORD, that he may have compassion on him, and to our God, for he will abundantly pardon.

Isaiah 57:21 There is no peace," says my God, "for the wicked."

Micah 7:18-19 Who is a God like you, pardoning iniquity and passing over transgression for the remnant of his inheritance? He does not retain his anger forever, because he delights in steadfast love. He

26

will again have compassion on us; he will tread our iniquities underfoot. You will cast all our sins into the depths of the sea.

John 14:27 Peace I leave with you; my peace I give to you. Not as the world gives do I give to you. Let not your hearts be troubled, neither let them be afraid.

Romans 5:1 Therefore, since we have been justified by faith, we have peace with God through our Lord Jesus Christ.

Romans 8:31-34 What then shall we say to these things? If God is for us, who can be against us? He who did not spare his own Son but gave him up for us all, how will he not also with him graciously give us all things? Who shall bring any charge against God's elect? It is God who justifies. Who is to condemn? Christ Jesus is the one who died—more than that, who was raised—who is at the right hand of God, who indeed is interceding for us.

Philippians 4:7 And the peace of God, which surpasses all understanding, will guard your hearts and your minds in Christ Jesus.

Chapter 6

FOR A NEW HEART—COME

"You must be born again," said Christ to Nicodemus. There must be a great change in our thoughts and feelings respecting God, before we are able to serve him on earth and enjoy him in heaven. Sin has estranged our minds from God, so that we do not desire him and love him. True religion is not pleasant to us. This is being "carnally minded, which is death." To love the things which sin makes distasteful is a great change, like coming to life. It is called the new birth, or regeneration. "Truly, truly, I say unto you, except a man be born again, he cannot see the kingdom of God."

Unconverted sinner, how can you expect to enter heaven? You would not be happy there. A swallow enjoys the air, and a cow the meadows, but a fish would soon languish there and die; there must be adaptation. Music charms those alone who have an ear for it; books are no treat to those who dislike reading; and society is only pleasant when it is congenial. A clown would not feel at ease at court, the ignorant cannot enjoy the company of the learned, the profligate do not love the society of the virtuous; and just so the ungodly cannot take pleasure in religion. Is not the Sabbath to you a dull day, the Bible a dry book, religious conversation unpleasant, prayer a task, and the company of the pious irksome? But heaven is all Sabbath, all worship, all holiness --its inhabitants all righteous; and their talk and actions all have reference to God. Heaven is happy because it is holy, and because God is there. But if you do not love holiness and God, it would not be a happy place for you. You would wander about a miserable, solitary thing, damping the enjoyment you could not share, and polluting the temple in which you alone would be made to worship. Therefore, unless born again, you never will enter.

You cannot, I know, change your own heart, but the Spirit of God can. And Jesus died to obtain for us the gift of the Spirit. And this gift is freely given to all who sincerely apply to the Savior for it. O then earnestly pray for the Spirit of God, that you may be born again. Come to Jesus with the petition of David, "Create in me a new heart, O God, and renew a right spirit within me." And for your encouragement, think of the gracious assurance of Christ, "If you, being evil, know how to give good gifts to your children, how much more shall your Father, which is in heaven, give the Holy Spirit to them that ask him?"

John 3:1-21 Now there was a man of the Pharisees named Nicodemus, a ruler of the Jews. This man came to Jesus by night and said to him, "Rabbi, we know that you are a teacher come from God, for no one can do these signs that you do unless God is with him." Jesus answered him, "Truly, truly, I say to you, unless one is born again he cannot see the kingdom of God." Nicodemus said to him, "How can a man be born when he is old? Can he enter a second time into his mother's womb and be born?" Jesus answered, "Truly, truly, I say to you, unless one is born of water and the Spirit, he cannot enter the kingdom of God. That which is born of the flesh is flesh, and that which is born of the Spirit is spirit. Do not marvel that I said to you, 'You must be born again.' The wind blows where it wishes, and you hear its sound, but you do not know where it comes from or where it goes. So it is with everyone who is born of the Spirit."

Nicodemus said to him, "How can these things be?" Jesus answered him, "Are you the teacher of Israel and yet you do not understand these things? Truly, truly, I say to you, we speak of what we know, and bear witness to what we have seen, but you do not receive our testimony. If I have told you earthly things and you do not believe, how can you believe if I tell you heavenly things?

No one has ascended into heaven except he who descended from heaven, the Son of Man. And as Moses lifted up the serpent in the wilderness, so must the Son of Man be lifted up, that whoever believes in him may have eternal life.

"For God so loved the world, that he gave his only Son, that whoever believes in him should not perish but have eternal life. For God did not send his Son into the world to condemn the world, but in order that the world might be saved through him.

Whoever believes in him is not condemned, but whoever does not believe is condemned already, because he has not believed in the name of the only Son of God. And this is the judgment: the light has come into the world, and people loved the darkness rather than the light because their works were evil. For everyone who does wicked things hates the light and does not come to the light, lest his works should be exposed. But whoever does what is true comes to the light, so that it may be clearly seen that his works have been carried out in God."

Romans 8:5-9 For those who live according to the flesh set their minds on the things of the flesh, but those who live according to the Spirit set their minds on the things of the Spirit. For to set the mind on the flesh is death, but to set the mind on the Spirit is life and peace. For the mind that is set on the flesh is hostile to God, for it does not submit to God's law; indeed, it cannot. Those who are in the flesh cannot please God. You, however, are not in the flesh but in the Spirit, if in fact the Spirit of God dwells in you. Anyone who does not have the Spirit of Christ does not belong to him.

Ephesians 2:1-6 And you were dead in the trespasses and sins in which you once walked, following the course of this world, following the prince of the power of the air, the spirit that is now at work in the sons of disobedience— among whom we all once lived in the passions of our flesh, carrying out the desires of the body and the mind, and were by nature children of wrath, like the rest of mankind. But God, being rich in mercy, because of the great love with which he loved us, even when we were dead in our trespasses, made us alive together with Christ—by grace you have been saved— and raised us up with him and seated us with him in the heavenly places in Christ Jesus,

Psalm 51:10-12 Create in me a clean heart, O God, and renew a right spirit within me. Cast me not away from your presence, and take not your Holy Spirit from me. Restore to me the joy of your salvation, and uphold me with a willing spirit.

Luke 11:1-13 Now Jesus was praying in a certain place, and when he finished, one of his disciples said to him, "Lord, teach us to pray, as John taught his disciples." And he said to them, "When you pray, say: "Father, hallowed be your name. Your kingdom come. Give us each day our daily bread, and forgive us our sins, for we ourselves forgive everyone who is indebted to us. And lead us not into temptation."

And he said to them, "Which of you who has a friend will go to him at midnight and say to him, 'Friend, lend me three loaves, for a friend of mine has arrived on a journey, and I have nothing to set before him'; and he will answer from within, 'Do not bother me; the door is now shut, and my children are with me in bed. I cannot get up and give you anything'? I tell you, though he will not get up and give him anything because he is his friend, yet because of his impudence he will rise and give him whatever he needs. And I tell you, ask, and it will be given to you; seek, and you will find; knock, and it will be opened to you. For everyone who asks receives, and the one who seeks finds, and to the one who knocks it will be opened. What father among you, if his son asks for a fish, will instead of a fish give him a serpent; or if he asks for an egg, will give him a scorpion? If you then, who are evil, know how to give good gifts to your children, how much more will the heavenly Father give the Holy Spirit to those who ask him!"

Chapter 7

FOR THE PRIVILEGES AND JOYS OF ADOPTION— COME

Persons who love children sometimes adopt unwanted children, and love and raise them as their own. And this is the way that God describes his treatment of those who come to Jesus. "You shall be my sons and daughters, says the Lord God Almighty." "We have received the Spirit of adoption, whereby we cry, Abba, Father." We are permitted, in prayer, to address God as "our Father, who is in heaven."

He loves these adopted children with more than an earthly parent's affection. He teaches, watches over, comforts, feeds, protects them. Sorrows are his kind chastisements, intended for their benefit. If you endure chastening, God deals with you as with sons; for whom the Lord loves, he chastens. In all their trials, he consoles them. "Like as a father pities his children, so the Lord pities them that fear him." "As one whom his mother comforts, so will I comfort you." Sickness, poverty, bereavement, all their troubles, are overruled for their advantage. "All things work together for good to them that love God." "They shall not want any good thing." "No weapon formed against them shall prosper." In every difficulty and danger their Father is at their side. "Fear not; for I have redeemed you. I have called you by your name; you are mine. When you pass through the waters, I will be with you; and through the rivers, they shall not overflow you." "I will never leave you nor forsake you."

They may tell their Father all their wants. "In everything make known your requests unto God." His ear is ever open to their cry, and his hand ever outstretched to do them good. As a Father, he provides for them an inheritance; but unlike those of earth, it is "incorruptible, undefiled, and fades not away.'

Oh what happiness to be a child of God; to feel "God is my Father! He loves me, pities, pardons, keeps me. I am safe from all evil. Wicked men and wicked spirits cannot harm me. God is my refuge, ever near; and he never slumbers, never is weary, never forgets, and will never change. He says, 'I have loved you with an everlasting love.' He will be always near me while on my journey here, and at last will take me to dwell with him in his palace forever." What earthly greatness can equal this?

Reader, would you be a child of God! You may, if you come to Jesus; for "as many as came to him, to them gave he power to become the sons of God."

Psalm 91:1-16 He who dwells in the shelter of the Most High will abide in the shadow of the Almighty. I will say to the LORD, "My refuge and my fortress, my God, in whom I trust." For he will deliver you from the snare of the fowler and from the deadly pestilence. He will cover you with his pinions, and under his wings you will find refuge; his faithfulness is a shield and buckler. You will not fear the terror of the night, nor the arrow that flies by day, nor the pestilence that stalks in darkness, nor the destruction that wastes at noonday. A thousand may fall at your side, ten thousand at your right hand, but it will not come near you. You will only look with your eyes and see the recompense of the wicked. Because you have made the LORD your dwelling place— the Most High, who is my refuge— no evil shall be allowed to befall you, no plague come near your tent. For he will command his angels concerning you to guard you in all your ways. On their hands they will bear you up, lest you strike your foot against a stone. You will tread on the lion and the adder; the young lion and the serpent you will trample underfoot.

"Because he holds fast to me in love, I will deliver him; I will protect him, because he knows my name. When he calls to me, I will answer him; I will be with him in trouble; I will rescue him and honor him. With long life I will satisfy him and show him my salvation."

John 1:12-13 But to all who did receive him, who believed in his name, he gave the right to become children of God, who were born, not of blood nor of the will of the flesh nor of the will of man, but of God.

Romans 8:14-17 For all who are led by the Spirit of God are sons of God. For you did not receive the spirit of slavery to fall back into fear, but you have received the Spirit of adoption as sons, by whom we cry, "Abba! Father!" The Spirit himself bears witness with our spirit that we are children of God, and if children, then heirs—heirs of God and fellow heirs with Christ, provided we suffer with him in order that we may also be glorified with him.

2 Corinthians 6:17-18 Therefore go out from their midst, and be separate from them, says the Lord, and touch no unclean thing; then I will welcome you, and I will be a father to you, and you shall be sons and daughters to me, says the Lord Almighty."

Hebrews 12:5-12 And have you forgotten the exhortation that addresses you as sons? "My son, do not regard lightly the discipline of the Lord, nor be weary when reproved by him. For the Lord disciplines the one he loves, and chastises every son whom he receives." It is for discipline that you have to endure. God is treating you as sons. For what son is there whom his father does not discipline? If you are left without discipline, in which all have participated, then you are illegitimate children and not sons. Besides this, we have had earthly fathers who disciplined us and we respected them. Shall we not much more be subject to the Father of spirits and live? For they disciplined us for a short time as it seemed best to them, but he disciplines us for our good, that we may share his holiness. For the moment all discipline seems painful rather than pleasant, but later it yields the peaceful fruit of righteousness to those who have been trained by it. Therefore lift your drooping hands and strengthen your weak knees,

1 John 3:1-2 See what kind of love the Father has given to us, that we should be called children of God; and so we are. The reason why

the world does not know us is that it did not know him. Beloved, we are God's children now, and what we will be has not yet appeared; but we know that when he appears we shall be like him, because we shall see him as he is.

Chapter 8

THAT YOU MAY ENTER HEAVEN—COME

As there is a place of punishment for the wicked, so there is a heaven of glory for all who come to Jesus. God, in his great love to sinners, sent his Son not only to deliver them from hell, but to make them happy and glorious with him forever. When a believer dies, though his body decays, his soul is at once with Jesus, which is "far better."

How delightful is the description the Bible gives of heaven. We are told that sickness, sorrow, and death never enter there; that cares, fears, and anxieties are never felt there; that poverty, privation, unkindness, and disappointment are never known there. The body that will rise from the grave will be "incorruptible," and will never experience pain, weariness, or decay. Old age will never enfeeble, for there will be perpetual youth; and death will never snatch away those we love, for death itself will be destroyed. What is still better, there will be no more sin, but all hearts will be full of holy love to God, and to one another. Every one will rejoice in the society and happiness of every one else, and God himself will dwell among them. All the good men of former ages will be there --the martyrs, and apostles, and prophets. There, too, we shall meet with angels and archangels; and more than all, we shall behold Jesus in his glorified human body--we shall see his face and ever be with the Lord.

To show how glorious heaven is, it is compared to a city with streets of gold, gates of pearl, and walls of jasper and emerald; to a paradise with a river clear as crystal, and the tree of life with healing leaves; to a place of rest after labor; to a father's house, a happy home. "They shall obtain joy and gladness, and sorrow and sighing shall flee away. Everlasting joy shall be upon their heads. In his presence is fullness of joy, and at his right hand are pleasures forevermore." "The best joys of earth are soon gone. Riches fly, health decays, friends depart, death is written on all things." But the joys of heaven are forever, and forever, and forever.

Reader, this heaven may be yours. Jesus keeps the door, but he has opened it wide for all sinners to enter. If you will not come to Jesus, you cannot enter heaven; for he is the door, the only door. But he invites you to come. Yes, however guilty and vile you are, heaven may, and certainly will be yours, if you come to Jesus. "To you is the word of this salvation sent." O, then, for heavenly bliss, come to Jesus.

John 14:1-6 "Let not your hearts be troubled. Believe in God; believe also in me. In my Father's house are many rooms. If it were not so, would I have told you that I go to prepare a place for you? And if I go and prepare a place for you, I will come again and will take you to myself, that where I am you may be also. And you know the way to where I am going." Thomas said to him, "Lord, we do not know where you are going. How can we know the way?" Jesus said to him, "I am the way, and the truth, and the life. No one comes to the Father except through me.

42

1 Corinthians 15:1-4 Now I would remind you, brothers, of the gospel I preached to you, which you received, in which you stand, and by which you are being saved, if you hold fast to the word I preached to you—unless you believed in vain.

For I delivered to you as of first importance what I also received: that Christ died for our sins in accordance with the Scriptures, that he was buried, that he was raised on the third day in accordance with the Scriptures,

1 Corinthians 15:12-26 Now if Christ is proclaimed as raised from the dead, how can some of you say that there is no resurrection of the dead? But if there is no resurrection of the dead, then not even Christ has been raised. And if Christ has not been raised, then our preaching is in vain and your faith is in vain. We are even found to be misrepresenting God, because we testified about God that he raised Christ, whom he did not raise if it is true that the dead are not raised. For if the dead are not raised, not even Christ has been raised. And if Christ has not been raised, your faith is futile and you are still in your sins. Then those also who have fallen asleep in Christ have perished. If in Christ we have hope in this life only, we are of all people most to be pitied.

But in fact Christ has been raised from the dead, the firstfruits of those who have fallen asleep. For as by a man came death, by a man has come also the resurrection of the dead. For as in Adam all die, so also in Christ shall all be made alive. But each in his own order: Christ the firstfruits, then at his coming those who belong to Christ. Then comes the end, when he delivers the kingdom to God the Father after destroying every rule and every authority and power. For he must reign until he has put all his enemies under his feet. The last enemy to be destroyed is death.

1 Corinthians 15:33-34 Do not be deceived: "Bad company ruins good morals." Wake up from your drunken stupor, as is right, and do not go on sinning. For some have no knowledge of God. I say this to your shame.

1 Corinthians 15:50-58 I tell you this, brothers: flesh and blood cannot inherit the kingdom of God, nor does the perishable inherit the imperishable. Behold! I tell you a mystery. We shall not all sleep, but we shall all be changed, in a moment, in the twinkling of an eye, at the last trumpet. For the trumpet will sound, and the dead will be raised imperishable, and we shall be changed. For this perishable body must put on the imperishable, and this mortal body must put on immortality. When the perishable puts on the imperishable, and the mortal puts on immortality, then shall come to pass the saying that is written: "Death is swallowed up in victory." "O death, where is your victory? O death, where is your sting?" The sting of death is sin, and the power of sin is the law. But thanks be to God, who gives us the victory through our Lord Jesus Christ.

Therefore, my beloved brothers, be steadfast, immovable, always abounding in the work of the Lord, knowing that in the Lord your labor is not in vain.

2 Corinthians 4:17-18 For this light momentary affliction is preparing for us an eternal weight of glory beyond all comparison, as we look not to the things that are seen but to the things that are unseen. For the things that are seen are transient, but the things that are unseen are eternal.

2 Corinthians 5:1-4 For we know that if the tent that is our earthly home is destroyed, we have a building from God, a house not made with hands, eternal in the heavens. For in this tent we groan, longing to put on our heavenly dwelling, if indeed by putting it on we may not be found naked. For while we are still in this tent, we groan, being burdened—not that we would be unclothed, but that we would be further clothed, so that what is mortal may be swallowed up by life.

Revelation 21:22 And I saw no temple in the city, for its temple is the Lord God the Almighty and the Lamb.

Chapter 9

WHO IS JESUS?

This is a most important inquiry, because no one can rightly comply with the invitation, "Come to Jesus," without a correct knowledge of who he is. Much depends on the answer we give to the question, "What do you think of Christ?"

JESUS IS GOD.

Before he appeared on earth, he had from eternity possessed all the perfections of Deity. As the Father is God, so also Jesus is God. This is a great mystery, but it is a great truth. The Bible clearly declares it. He is called "The Word;" and John tells us, "In the beginning was the Word, and the Word was with God, and the Word was God. All things were made by him, and without him was not anything made that was made." And "The Word was made flesh, and dwelt among us." Speaking of himself, Jesus said, "Before Abraham was, I am." He referred to the "glory which he had with the Father before the world began;" and declared, "I and the Father are one." We are told that he is "the brightness of the Father's glory," "the image of the invisible God," "God manifest in the flesh;" that "he is the same yesterday, today and for ever;" and that "in him dwells all the fulness of the Godhead bodily." Jesus, therefore, is God; and is perfect in power and wisdom and goodness. There is nothing he cannot do; and as he never can change, he will never be unfaithful to his promises.

Now, poor sinner, this is just such a Savior as you want. If you needed a protector from some great danger you would go to some one who was mighty. Who is as mighty as Jesus? All that God can do, he can do. There are no difficulties, dangers, or foes he is unable to conquer for you. Whatever your weakness, his strength must be all sufficient. It is not some frail fellow-man, it is not even an angel you are to trust in. It is one infinitely higher than all created beings --even the great God, mighty to save. We should have cause to fear, if any one inferior were our Savior. But we may feel quite safe when he undertakes to save, he who is the Lord of heaven and earth. Who can harm us, if he promises to help us? "If God be for us, who can be against us?"-- His power, wisdom, holiness, and goodness, are all employed on our behalf, --as soon as we come to Jesus. With such a Savior we cannot perish. "He is able to save to the UTTERMOST."

John 1:1-3 In the beginning was the Word, and the Word was with God, and the Word was God. He was in the beginning with God. All things were made through him, and without him was not any thing made that was made.

John 1:14 And the Word became flesh and dwelt among us, and we have seen his glory, glory as of the only Son from the Father, full of grace and truth.

John 8:58 Jesus said to them, "Truly, truly, I say to you, before Abraham was, I am."

John 10:30 "I and the Father are one."

John 17:5 And now, Father, glorify me in your own presence with the glory that I had with you before the world existed.

Colossians 1:14-20 In whom we have redemption, the forgiveness of sins. He is the image of the invisible God, the firstborn of all creation. For by him all things were created, in heaven and on earth, visible and invisible, whether thrones or dominions or rulers or authorities—all things were created through him and for him. And he is before all things, and in him all things hold together. And he is the head of the body, the church. He is the beginning, the firstborn from the dead, that in everything he might be preeminent. For in him all the fullness of God was pleased to dwell, and through him to reconcile to himself all things, whether on earth or in heaven, making peace by the blood of his cross.

Colossians 2:9 For in him the whole fullness of deity dwells bodily,

1 Timothy 3:16 Great indeed, we confess, is the mystery of godliness: He was manifested in the flesh, vindicated by the Spirit, seen by angels, proclaimed among the nations, believed on in the world, taken up in glory.

Hebrews 1:1-14 Long ago, at many times and in many ways, God spoke to our fathers by the prophets, but in these last days he has spoken to us by his Son, whom he appointed the heir of all things, through whom also he created the world. He is the radiance of the glory of God and the exact imprint of his nature, and he upholds the universe by the word of his power. After making purification for sins, he sat down at the right hand of the Majesty on high, having become as much superior to angels as the name he has inherited is more excellent than theirs.

For to which of the angels did God ever say, "You are my Son, today I have begotten you"? Or again, "I will be to him a father, and he shall be to me a son"? And again, when he brings the firstborn into the world, he says, "Let all God's angels worship him." Of the angels he says, "He makes his angels winds, and his ministers a flame of fire." But of the Son he says, "Your throne, O God, is forever and ever, the scepter of uprightness is the scepter of your kingdom. You have loved righteousness and hated wickedness; therefore God, your God, has anointed you with the oil of gladness beyond your companions." And, "You, Lord, laid the foundation of the earth in the beginning, and the heavens are the work of your hands; they will perish, but you remain; they will all wear out like a garment, like a robe you will roll them up, like a garment they will be changed. But you are the same, and your years will have no end." And to which of the angels has he ever said, "Sit at my right hand until I make your enemies a footstool for your feet"? Are they not all ministering spirits sent out to serve for the sake of those who are to inherit salvation?

Hebrews 7:23-28 The former priests were many in number, because they were prevented by death from continuing in office, but he holds his priesthood permanently, because he continues forever. Consequently, he is able to save to the uttermost those who draw near to God through him, since he always lives to make intercession for them.

For it was indeed fitting that we should have such a high priest, holy, innocent, unstained, separated from sinners, and exalted above the heavens. He has no need, like those high priests, to offer sacrifices daily, first for his own sins and then for those of the people, since he did this once for all when he offered up himself. For the law appoints men in their weakness as high priests, but the word of the oath, which came later than the law, appoints a Son who has been made perfect forever.

Hebrews 13:8 Jesus Christ is the same yesterday and today and forever.

Chapter 10

JESUS IS MAN

This is as true as that he is God. "God so loved the world that he sent his only begotten Son." And Jesus, though "equal with God," "took upon him the form of a servant, and was made in the likeness of men, and was found in fashion as a man." He was predicted as "a man of sorrows," and frequently spoke of himself as "the Son of man." He became man in order to obey the law we had broken, and to suffer the punishment we had earned. Because no one can see God, Jesus lived among us as a man, that from his spirit and conduct we might have a clearer idea of what God is. Thus he said "He that has seen me, has seen the Father." And he became a man that, suffering what we suffer, we might feel sure that he can sympathize with us. Thus we read, "In that he himself has suffered, being tempted, he is able to minister to those that are tempted;" and, "For we do not have a high priest who is unable to sympathize with our weaknesses, but one who in every respect has been tempted as we are, yet without sin."

Think, then, of Jesus as a man. Just over there is a funeral. It is a widow's only son, and she follows the corpse with a broken heart. Who is the man that sees her afar off, pities her, goes up to the dead body, restores it to life, and delivers the son to his mother? That loving but mighty man is Jesus. Who is this standing amid a crowd of little children, and taking them so kindly in his arms to bless them? It is

Jesus. Who is that mourner weeping at the grave of Lazarus? It is Jesus. Who is it that all the sick, and the poor, and the sorrowful run after, and who heals and comforts them all, refusing none? It is Jesus. He is still the same; a loving, tender, compassionate man.

You need not be afraid of him; he is a man, your brother. It is he who says to you, "Come unto me." Listen to him, sinner. He is the mighty God, and able to save you; but he is also the "man of sorrows," and full of sympathy and love. He knows, feels, and pities all your weakness and frailties and fears. He tells you to not be afraid. As a brother-man, he stands with looks of unutterable kindness, and says, "come unto me, come unto me." Do not be indifferent to such a loving Friend. Listen to him. Let your heart be touched by his tenderness. Trust in his promises. Come to Jesus at once. Rely on him as your Savior, and obey him as your King, and he will be to you the "Friend that sticks closer than a brother."

John 11:32-45 Now when Mary came to where Jesus was and saw him, she fell at his feet, saying to him, "Lord, if you had been here, my brother would not have died." When Jesus saw her weeping, and the Jews who had come with her also weeping, he was deeply moved in his spirit and greatly troubled. And he said, "Where have you laid him?" They said to him, "Lord, come and see." Jesus wept. So the Jews said, "See how he loved him!" But some of them said, "Could not he who opened the eyes of the blind man also have kept this man from dying?"

Then Jesus, deeply moved again, came to the tomb. It was a cave, and a stone lay against it. Jesus said, "Take away the stone." Martha, the sister of the dead man, said to him, "Lord, by this time there will be an odor, for he has been dead four days." Jesus said to her, "Did I not tell you that if you believed you would see the glory of God?" So they took away the stone.

And Jesus lifted up his eyes and said, "Father, I thank you that you have heard me. I knew that you always hear me, but I said this on account of the people standing around, that they may believe that you sent me."

When he had said these things, he cried out with a loud voice, "Lazarus, come out." The man who had died came out, his hands and feet bound with linen strips, and his face wrapped with a cloth. Jesus said to them, "Unbind him, and let him go." Many of the Jews therefore, who had come with Mary and had seen what he did, believed in him,

Luke 7:11-15 Soon afterward he went to a town called Nain, and his disciples and a great crowd went with him. As he drew near to the gate of the town, behold, a man who had died was being carried out, the only son of his mother, and she was a widow, and a considerable crowd from the town was with her. And when the Lord saw her, he had compassion on her and said to her, "Do not weep." Then he came up and touched the bier, and the bearers stood still. And he said, "Young man, I say to you, arise." And the dead man sat up and began to speak, and Jesus gave him to his mother.

Isaiah 53:1-12 Who has believed what he has heard from us? And to whom has the arm of the LORD been revealed?

For he grew up before him like a young plant, and like a root out of dry ground; he had no form or majesty that we should look at him, and no beauty that we should desire him. He was despised and rejected by men; a man of sorrows, and acquainted with grief; and as one from whom men hide their faces he was despised, and we esteemed him not.

Surely he has borne our griefs and carried our sorrows; yet we esteemed him stricken, smitten by God, and afflicted. But he was pierced for our transgressions; he was crushed for our iniquities; upon him was the chastisement that brought us peace, and with his wounds we are healed. All we like sheep have gone astray; we have turned—every one—to his own way; and the LORD has laid on him the iniquity of us all. He was oppressed, and he was afflicted, yet he opened not his mouth; like a lamb that is led to the slaughter, and like a sheep that before its shearers is silent, so he opened not his mouth. By oppression and judgment he was taken away; and as for his generation, who considered that he was cut off out of the land of the living, stricken for the transgression of my people? And they made his grave with the wicked and with a rich man in his death, although he had done no violence, and there was no deceit in his mouth.

Yet it was the will of the LORD to crush him; he has put him to grief; when his soul makes an offering for guilt, he shall see his offspring; he shall prolong his days; the will of the LORD shall prosper in his hand. Out of the anguish of his soul he shall see and be satisfied; by his knowledge shall the righteous one, my servant, make many to be accounted righteous, and he shall bear their iniquities.

Therefore I will divide him a portion with the many, and he shall divide the spoil with the strong, because he poured out his soul to death and was numbered with the transgressors; yet he bore the sin of many, and makes intercession for the transgressors.

Matthew 26:1-2 When Jesus had finished all these sayings, he said to his disciples, "You know that after two days the Passover is coming, and the Son of Man will be delivered up to be crucified."

Matthew 27:2 When morning came, all the chief priests and the elders of the people took counsel against Jesus to put him to death. And they bound him and led him away and delivered him over to Pilate the governor.

Matthew 27:11-14 Now Jesus stood before the governor, and the governor asked him, "Are you the King of the Jews?" Jesus said, "You have said so." But when he was accused by the chief priests and elders, he gave no answer. Then Pilate said to him, "Do you not hear how many things they testify against you?" But he gave him no answer, not even to a single charge, so that the governor was greatly amazed.

Matthew 27:27-31 Then the soldiers of the governor took Jesus into the governor's headquarters, and they gathered the whole battalion before him. And they stripped him and put a scarlet robe on him, and twisting together a crown of thorns, they put it on his head and put a reed in his right hand. And kneeling before him, they mocked him, saying, "Hail, King of the Jews!" And they spit on him and took the reed and struck him on the head. And when they had mocked him, they stripped him of the robe and put his own clothes on him and led him away to crucify him.

Matthew 27:45-51 Now from the sixth hour there was darkness over all the land until the ninth hour. And about the ninth hour Jesus cried out with a loud voice, saying, "Eli, Eli, lema sabachthani?" that is, "My God, my God, why have you forsaken me?" And some of the bystanders, hearing it, said, "This man is calling Elijah." And one of them at once ran and took a sponge, filled it with sour wine, and put it on a reed and gave it to him to drink. But the others said, "Wait, let us see whether Elijah will come to save him."

And Jesus cried out again with a loud voice and yielded up his spirit. And behold, the curtain of the temple was torn in two, from top to bottom. And the earth shook, and the rocks were split.

Matthew 27:54 When the centurion and those who were with him, keeping watch over Jesus, saw the earthquake and what took place, they were filled with awe and said, "Truly this was the Son of God!"

Matthew 27:58-66 He (Joseph of Arimathea) went to Pilate and asked for the body of Jesus. Then Pilate ordered it to be given to him. And Joseph took the body and wrapped it in a clean linen shroud and laid it in his own new tomb, which he had cut in the rock. And he rolled a great stone to the entrance of the tomb and went away. Mary Magdalene and the other Mary were there, sitting opposite the tomb.

The next day, that is, after the day of Preparation, the chief priests and the Pharisees gathered before Pilate and said, "Sir, we remember how that impostor said, while he was still alive, 'After three days I will rise.' Therefore order the tomb to be made secure until the third day, lest his disciples go and steal him away and tell the people, 'He has risen from the dead,' and the last fraud will be worse than the first." Pilate said to them, "You have a guard of soldiers. Go, make it as secure as you can." So they went and made the tomb secure by sealing the stone and setting a guard.

Matthew 28:1-8 Now after the Sabbath, toward the dawn of the first day of the week, Mary Magdalene and the other Mary went to see the tomb. And behold, there was a great earthquake, for an angel of the Lord descended from heaven and came and rolled back the stone and sat on it. His appearance was like lightning, and his clothing white as snow. And for fear of him the guards trembled and became like dead men.

But the angel said to the women, "Do not be afraid, for I know that you seek Jesus who was crucified. He is not here, for he has risen, as he said. Come, see the place where he lay. Then go quickly and tell his disciples that he has risen from the dead, and behold, he is going before you to Galilee; there you will see him. See, I have told you."

So they departed quickly from the tomb with fear and great joy, and ran to tell his disciples.

John 3:16-17 "For God so loved the world, that he gave his only Son, that whoever believes in him should not perish but have eternal life. For God did not send his Son into the world to condemn the world, but in order that the world might be saved through him.

Philippians 2:5-11 Have this mind among yourselves, which is yours in Christ Jesus, who, though he was in the form of God, did not count equality with God a thing to be grasped, but emptied himself, by taking the form of a servant, being born in the likeness of men. And being found in human form, he humbled himself by becoming obedient to the point of death, even death on a cross. Therefore God has highly exalted him and bestowed on him the name that is above every name, so that at the name of Jesus every knee should bow, in heaven and on earth and under the earth, and every tongue confess that Jesus Christ is Lord, to the glory of God the Father.

Hebrews 2:17-18 Therefore he had to be made like his brothers in every respect, so that he might become a merciful and faithful high priest in the service of God, to make propitiation for the sins of the people. For because he himself has suffered when tempted, he is able to help those who are being tempted.

Chapter 11

HE IS THE SAVIOR OF SINNERS

The saying is trustworthy and deserving of full acceptance, that Christ Jesus came into the world to save **SINNERS.** -- "God exalted him at his right hand as Prince and Savior." This alone brought him to our wicked world.

And how does he save? By standing in our place, and bearing the punishment we earned and deserved. We have broken the law, but he has perfectly kept it; for he was holy, sinless, undefiled, separate from sinners. We deserved death for our sins. "The soul that sins shall die." But he died for us. "He gave his life a ransom for many." We were under the curse. "Cursed is every one who does not do all things written in the book of the law." But "he was made a curse for us." "He was pierced for our transgressions; he was crushed for our iniquities; upon him was the chastisement that brought us peace, and with his wounds we are healed." "He himself bore our sins in his body on the tree, that we might die to sin and live to righteousness."

This is why he became a man, was "despised and rejected, a man of sorrows, and acquainted with grief." He "carried our sorrows." This is why he suffered temptation, groaned in Gethsemane, in his agony sweat great drops of blood, was scourged, spit upon, crowned with thorns, and nailed upon the cross. "He gave his life a ransom for many." We were slaves--he came to set us free. But the price he paid was his own blood. "Redeemed with the precious blood of Christ." We were prisoners at the bar, condemned to die; but he left his Father's throne, and came and stood at our side, saying, "I will die for them, that they may be forgiven and live for ever."

And now that he has returned to his glory in heaven, he lives to save us. He watches over us, speaks to us by his word and by his Spirit, listens to our prayers, advocates our cause, helps us in our weakness, and "ever lives to make intercession for us." He thus saves us both by his death and his life. He has paid all our sin debts, and is ready to supply all our wants. He saves those who trust in him from the sting of death, and delivers them from condemnation at the judgment day.

He says to you, reader, "Poor sinner, you are in danger of hell; but I have brought you a free pardon, purchased with my own blood. I died for you. I am able to save you. Come unto me."

Acts 10:34-43 So Peter opened his mouth and said: "Truly I understand that God shows no partiality, but in every nation anyone who fears him and does what is right is acceptable to him. As for the word that he sent to Israel, preaching good news of peace through Jesus Christ (he is Lord of all), you yourselves know what happened throughout all Judea, beginning from Galilee after the baptism that John proclaimed: how God anointed Jesus of Nazareth with the Holy Spirit and with power. He went about doing good and healing all who were oppressed by the devil, for God was with him. And we are witnesses of all that he did both in the country of the Jews and in

Jerusalem. They put him to death by hanging him on a tree, but God raised him on the third day and made him to appear, not to all the people but to us who had been chosen by God as witnesses, who ate and drank with him after he rose from the dead. And he commanded us to preach to the people and to testify that he is the one appointed by God to be judge of the living and the dead. To him all the prophets bear witness that everyone who believes in him receives forgiveness of sins through his name."

Acts 13:16-41 So Paul stood up, and motioning with his hand said: "Men of Israel and you who fear God, listen. The God of this people Israel chose our fathers and made the people great during their stay in the land of Egypt, and with uplifted arm he led them out of it. And for about forty years he put up with them in the wilderness. And after destroying seven nations in the land of Canaan, he gave them their land as an inheritance. All this took about 450 years. And after that he gave them judges until Samuel the prophet.

Then they asked for a king, and God gave them Saul the son of Kish, a man of the tribe of Benjamin, for forty years. And when he had removed him, he raised up David to be their king, of whom he testified and said, 'I have found in David the son of Jesse a man after my heart, who will do all my will.' Of this man's offspring God has brought to Israel a Savior, Jesus, as he promised. Before his coming, John had proclaimed a baptism of repentance to all the people of Israel. And as John was finishing his course, he said, 'What do you suppose that I am? I am not he. No, but behold, after me one is coming, the sandals of whose feet I am not worthy to untie.'

"Brothers, sons of the family of Abraham, and those among you who fear God, to us has been sent the message of this salvation. For those who live in Jerusalem and their rulers, because they did not recognize him nor understand the utterances of the prophets, which are read every Sabbath, fulfilled them by condemning him. And though they found in him no guilt worthy of death, they asked Pilate to have him executed. And when they had carried out all that was written of him, they took him down from the tree and laid him in a tomb. But God raised him from the dead, and for many days he appeared to those who had come up with him from Galilee to Jerusalem, who are now his witnesses to the people.

And we bring you the good news that what God promised to the fathers, this he has fulfilled to us their children by raising Jesus, as also it is written in the second Psalm, "'You are my Son, today I have begotten you.' And as for the fact that he raised him from the dead, no more to return to corruption, he has spoken in this way, "'I will give you the holy and sure blessings of David.' Therefore he says also in another psalm, "'You will not let your Holy One see corruption.' For David, after he had served the purpose of God in his own generation, fell asleep and was laid with his fathers and saw corruption, but he whom God raised up did not see corruption. Let it be known to you therefore, brothers, that through this man forgiveness of sins is proclaimed to you, and by him everyone who believes is freed from everything from which you could not be freed by the law of Moses.

Beware, therefore, lest what is said in the Prophets should come about: "'Look, you scoffers, be astounded and perish; for I am doing a work in your days, a work that you will not believe, even if one tells it to you.'"

Romans 5:1-21 Therefore, since we have been justified by faith, we have peace with God through our Lord Jesus Christ. Through him we have also obtained access by faith into this grace in which we stand, and we rejoice in hope of the glory of God. Not only that, but we rejoice in our sufferings, knowing that suffering produces endurance, and endurance produces character, and character produces hope, and hope does not put us to shame, because God's love has been poured into our hearts through the Holy Spirit who has been given to us.

For while we were still weak, at the right time Christ died for the ungodly. For one will scarcely die for a righteous person—though perhaps for a good person one would dare even to die— but God shows his love for us in that while we were still sinners, Christ died for us. Since, therefore, we have now been justified by his blood, much more shall we be saved by him from the wrath of God. For if while we were enemies we were reconciled to God by the death of his Son, much more, now that we are reconciled, shall we be saved by his life. More than that, we also rejoice in God through our Lord Jesus Christ, through whom we have now received reconciliation.

Therefore, just as sin came into the world through one man, and death through sin, and so death spread to all men because all sinned— for sin indeed was in the world before the law was given, but sin is not counted where there is no law. Yet death reigned from Adam to Moses, even over those whose sinning was not like the transgression of Adam, who was a type of the one who was to come.

But the free gift is not like the trespass. For if many died through one man's trespass, much more have the grace of God and the free gift by the grace of that one man Jesus Christ abounded for many. And the free gift is not like the result of that one man's sin. For the judgment following one trespass brought condemnation, but the free gift following many trespasses brought justification. For if, because of one man's trespass, death reigned through that one man, much more will those who receive the abundance of grace and the free gift of righteousness reign in life through the one man Jesus Christ.

Therefore, as one trespass led to condemnation for all men, so one act of righteousness leads to justification and life for all men. For as by the one man's disobedience the many were made sinners, so by the one man's obedience the many will be made righteous.

Now the law came in to increase the trespass, but where sin increased, grace abounded all the more, so that, as sin reigned in death, grace also might reign through righteousness leading to eternal life through Jesus Christ our Lord.

Galatians 3:13 Christ redeemed us from the curse of the law by becoming a curse for us—for it is written, "Cursed is everyone who is hanged on a tree"—

1 Timothy 1:15 The saying is trustworthy and deserving of full acceptance, that Christ Jesus came into the world to save sinners, of whom I am the foremost.

Hebrews 9:11-28 But when Christ appeared as a high priest of the good things that have come, then through the greater and more perfect tent (not made with hands, that is, not of this creation) he entered once for all into the holy places, not by means of the blood of goats and calves but by means of his own blood, thus securing an eternal redemption. For if the blood of goats and bulls, and the sprinkling of defiled persons with the ashes of a heifer, sanctify for the purification of the flesh, how much more will the blood of Christ, who through the eternal Spirit offered himself without blemish to God, purify our conscience from dead works to serve the living God.

Therefore he is the mediator of a new covenant, so that those who are called may receive the promised eternal inheritance, since a death has occurred that redeems them from the transgressions committed under the first covenant. For where a will is involved, the death of the one who made it must be established. For a will takes effect only at death, since it is not in force as long as the one who made it is alive. Therefore not even the first covenant was inaugurated without blood. For when every commandment of the law had been declared by Moses to all the people, he took the blood of calves and goats, with water and scarlet wool and hyssop, and sprinkled both the book itself and all the people, saying, "This is the blood of the covenant that God commanded for you." And in the same way he sprinkled with the blood both the tent and all the vessels used in worship. Indeed, under the law almost everything is purified with blood, and without the shedding of blood there is no forgiveness of sins.

Thus it was necessary for the copies of the heavenly things to be purified with these rites, but the heavenly things themselves with better sacrifices than these. For Christ has entered, not into holy places made with hands, which are copies of the true things, but into heaven itself, now to appear in the presence of God on our behalf. Nor was it to offer himself repeatedly, as the high priest enters the holy places every year with blood not his own, for then he would have had to suffer repeatedly since the foundation of the world. But as it is, he has appeared once for all at the end of the ages to put away sin by the sacrifice of himself. And just as it is appointed for man to die once, and after that comes judgment, so Christ, having been offered once to bear the sins of many, will appear a second time, not to deal with sin but to save those who are eagerly waiting for him.

1 Peter 1:18-19 knowing that you were ransomed from the futile ways inherited from your forefathers, not with perishable things such as silver or gold, but with the precious blood of Christ, like that of a lamb without blemish or spot.

Chapter 12

HE IS THE ONLY SAVIOR

Jesus said, "I am the way: no one comes to the Father but by ME." We can only obtain pardon from God by coming to Jesus for it. All God's mercy for sinners has been placed in the hand of Christ, and no one can obtain it but from him.

Some neglect Jesus, yet hope in God's mercy to get them to God. But if they reject Jesus, they reject mercy. To them God will only be an angry Judge, "a consuming fire." Our own good works cannot save us. Our best actions are sinful; and if they were perfect, they could not atone for the past. St. Paul says, "For by works of the law no human being will be justified in his sight." If we could have entered heaven by our own merits, why should Christ have died? We could have saved ourselves. O trust not in your own works, your good character, your honesty and charity--nothing but the righteousness and death of Jesus can save.

Some think because they have been baptized and taken the sacrament, because they read their Bible, keep the Sabbath, and go to church they will be saved. Multitudes have done this, yet, having never come to Jesus, are now in hell. No sacrament, ceremony, creed, or church can save. None but Jesus can.

Some rely on their priest. Sad mistake. Poor man, he needs a Savior for himself. He cannot save his own soul, much less yours.

None but Jesus can give absolution. His blood alone cleanses from sin. Some pray to saints, angels, and the Virgin Mary; but who can tell whether they can listen to any who address them? and if they could can they save the soul?

The Bible tells us plainly, "There is one mediator between God and men, the man Christ Jesus." "Neither is there salvation in any other; for there is none other name under heaven given among men, whereby we must be saved." Look then to no one else. Trust only in Jesus. He is seated on a throne of mercy, and invites all poor sinners to come at once close up to him. He alone has pardon to give. Why then stop to talk to fellow sinners, or even angels, when no being can help you but Jesus? You need no one to introduce you to him. The beggar and the prince, the black man, and the white, the ignorant and the learned, those clothed in rags and those in silk attire, are equally welcome. All are invited. You sin by looking anywhere else for help. He says, "look unto me, and be saved, all the ends of the earth." Look away from men, away from yourself; look only to Jesus, for he alone can save.

Acts 4:8-12 Then Peter, filled with the Holy Spirit, said to them, "Rulers of the people and elders, if we are being examined today concerning a good deed done to a crippled man, by what means this man has been healed, let it be known to all of you and to all the people of Israel that by the name of Jesus Christ of Nazareth, whom you crucified, whom God raised from the dead—by him this man is standing before you well. This Jesus is the stone that was rejected by you, the builders, which has become the cornerstone. And there is salvation in no one else, for there is no other name under heaven given among men by which we must be saved."

Romans 3:20-28 For by works of the law no human being will be justified in his sight, since through the law comes knowledge of sin.

But now the righteousness of God has been manifested apart from the law, although the Law and the Prophets bear witness to it— the righteousness of God through faith in Jesus Christ for all who believe. For there is no distinction: for all have sinned and fall short of the glory of God, and are justified by his grace as a gift, through the redemption that is in Christ Jesus, whom God put forward as a propitiation by his blood, to be received by faith. This was to show God's righteousness, because in his divine forbearance he had passed over former sins. It was to show his righteousness at the present time, so that he might be just and the justifier of the one who has faith in Jesus.

Then what becomes of our boasting? It is excluded. By what kind of law? By a law of works? No, but by the law of faith. For we hold that one is justified by faith apart from works of the law.

Galatians 2:16 yet we know that a person is not justified by works of the law but through faith in Jesus Christ, so we also have believed in Christ Jesus, in order to be justified by faith in Christ and not by works of the law, because by works of the law no one will be justified.

71

Philippians 3:9 and be found in him, not having a righteousness of my own that comes from the law, but that which comes through faith in Christ, the righteousness from God that depends on faith—

1 Timothy 2:5-6 For there is one God, and there is one mediator between God and men, the man Christ Jesus, who gave himself as a ransom for all, which is the testimony given at the proper time.

Chapter 13

HE IS A LOVING SAVIOR

There could be no stronger proof of this than his coming from heaven to suffer and to die. His own words were "Greater love has no man than this, that a man lay down his life for his friends." Why did he leave a holy heaven for a sinful world; the songs of angels for the temptations of devils, a throne of glory for a cross of agony? It was love only, only love. Love, not to friends but to enemies. "While we were yet sinners, Christ died for us."

He showed his tender love in a thousand ways when on earth, going about doing good, healing all manner of sickness, never turning from the poor and the sad, always the "Friend of sinners." How he wept over Jerusalem, as he thought of her sins and approaching sufferings. When in the agonies of death, how kindly he spoke to the penitent thief at his side; and how earnestly he prayed for his mocking murderers: "Father, forgive them; for they know not what they do." He might easily have called forth an army of angels to deliver him; but if he had not died, we could not have been saved: and therefore, because he loved us, he drank the bitter cup to its very dregs. Now that he has risen again, his love to sinners is as great as ever. Love prompts him to intercede for us, to pity us, to send his Spirit to help us, and saves us.

He loves you; he died for you; he looks down with pity on you; he calls you to come to him. His love has spared you till now, though you have rejected him. His love bears with your sins, and again at this moment entreats you to accept a pardon purchased by his blood. If some friend had spent his fortune to deliver you from prison, or risked his life to save yours, could you treat him with neglect? But Jesus has done far more. He died to redeem you from eternal misery and suffering, and make you happy for ever in heaven. He comes to you, and showing the marks of his wounds, he says, "See how I loved you, sinner. I love you still. Come unto me, that I may save you from sin and from hell."

Do not reject such a gracious Savior. Trample not under feet such wonderful love. You will never meet with another Friend like this One. Trust him. Love him. You will always find him full of pity and tenderness. He will comfort, guide, protect, and save you amid all the dangers and sorrows of life, deliver you from the sting of death, and then make you happy for ever in heaven. O come to this loving Savior.

Luke 19:41-44 And when he drew near and saw the city, he wept over it, saying, "Would that you, even you, had known on this day the things that make for peace! But now they are hidden from your eyes. For the days will come upon you, when your enemies will set up a barricade around you and surround you and hem you in on every side and tear you down to the ground, you and your children within you. And they will not leave one stone upon another in you, because you did not know the time of your visitation."

Luke 23:33-43 And when they came to the place that is called The Skull, there they crucified him, and the criminals, one on his right and one on his left. And Jesus said, "Father, forgive them, for they know not what they do." And they cast lots to divide his garments.

And the people stood by, watching, but the rulers scoffed at him, saying, "He saved others; let him save himself, if he is the Christ of God, his Chosen One!" The soldiers also mocked him, coming up and offering him sour wine and saying, "If you are the King of the Jews, save yourself!" There was also an inscription over him, "This is the King of the Jews."

One of the criminals who were hanged railed at him, saying, "Are you not the Christ? Save yourself and us!" But the other rebuked him, saying, "Do you not fear God, since you are under the same sentence of condemnation? And we indeed justly, for we are receiving the due reward of our deeds; but this man has done nothing wrong." And he said, "Jesus, remember me when you come into your kingdom." And he said to him, "Truly, I say to you, today you will be with me in Paradise."

John 10:1-30 "Truly, truly, I say to you, he who does not enter the sheepfold by the door but climbs in by another way, that man is a thief and a robber. But he who enters by the door is the shepherd of the sheep. To him the gatekeeper opens. The sheep hear his voice, and he calls his own sheep by name and leads them out. When he has brought out all his own, he goes before them, and the sheep follow him, for they know his voice. A stranger they will not follow, but they will flee from him, for they do not know the voice of strangers."

This figure of speech Jesus used with them, but they did not understand what he was saying to them.

So Jesus again said to them, "Truly, truly, I say to you, I am the door of the sheep. All who came before me are thieves and robbers, but the sheep did not listen to them. I am the door. If anyone enters by me, he will be saved and will go in and out and find pasture.

The thief comes only to steal and kill and destroy. I came that they may have life and have it abundantly. I am the good shepherd. The good shepherd lays down his life for the sheep. He who is a hired hand and not a shepherd, who does not own the sheep, sees the wolf coming and leaves the sheep and flees, and the wolf snatches them and scatters them. He flees because he is a hired hand and cares nothing for the sheep.

I am the good shepherd. I know my own and my own know me, just as the Father knows me and I know the Father; and I lay down my life for the sheep. And I have other sheep that are not of this fold. I must bring them also, and they will listen to my voice. So there will be one flock, one shepherd. For this reason the Father loves me, because I lay down my life that I may take it up again. No one takes it from me, but I lay it down of my own accord. I have authority to lay it down, and I have authority to take it up again. This charge I have received from my Father."

There was again a division among the Jews because of these words. Many of them said, "He has a demon, and is insane; why listen to

76

him?" Others said, "These are not the words of one who is oppressed by a demon. Can a demon open the eyes of the blind?"

At that time the Feast of Dedication took place at Jerusalem. It was winter, and Jesus was walking in the temple, in the colonnade of Solomon. So the Jews gathered around him and said to him, "How long will you keep us in suspense? If you are the Christ, tell us plainly." Jesus answered them, "I told you, and you do not believe. The works that I do in my Father's name bear witness about me, but you do not believe because you are not among my sheep. My sheep hear my voice, and I know them, and they follow me. I give them eternal life, and they will never perish, and no one will snatch them out of my hand. My Father, who has given them to me, is greater than all, and no one is able to snatch them out of the Father's hand. I and the Father are one."

John 15:12-15 "This is my commandment, that you love one another as I have loved you. Greater love has no one than this, that someone lay down his life for his friends. You are my friends if you do what I command you. No longer do I call you servants, for the servant does not know what his master is doing; but I have called you friends, for all that I have heard from my Father I have made known to you.

Romans 5:6-8 For while we were still weak, at the right time Christ died for the ungodly. For one will scarcely die for a righteous person —though perhaps for a good person one would dare even to die— but

God shows his love for us in that while we were still sinners, Christ died for us.

Ephesians 3:17-19 so that Christ may dwell in your hearts through faith—that you, being rooted and grounded in love, may have strength to comprehend with all the saints what is the breadth and length and height and depth, and to know the love of Christ that surpasses knowledge, that you may be filled with all the fullness of God.

Chapter 14

HE WILL BE OUR JUDGE

"We must all appear before the judgment seat of Christ." The man of sorrows will come again as the God of glory, and "before him will be gathered all nations." "Behold, he is coming with the clouds, and every eye will see him, even those who pierced him."

How encouraging to believers. He is the very person they would have chosen for themselves, and when they see him on the throne they will rejoice, for their best Friend, who has promised to save them, will be their Judge, and therefore they will feel secure. But how dreadful for those who have rejected him. How terrible his look of reproach to those who pierced him by their sinful neglect. How dreadful to hear the voice which now says, "Come unto me," say, "Depart, you cursed."

Suppose a prisoner is soon to be tried for a crime for which he will lose his life. He is visited by a man of humble appearance, but great kindness, whose heart seems to overflow with pity for the prisoner. He has been laboring very hard for the culprit's release at the trial. He tells him what he has done, and proves that he may be safely trusted. He assures him that he is quite able to secure his acquittal or his pardon, if only the prisoner is willing he should do so. He says, "I beg you let me come forward at the trial, and speak on your behalf. Let me plead your cause. I have saved many a prisoner whose case was as bad as yours; I can save you. I ask no payment. Love alone prompts me. Consent to let me help you." But the prisoner is reading, talking, or sleeping, and takes no notice of this friend. He comes again and again; but the prisoner dislikes his visits, and by his actions asks him not to come and disturb him. The trial comes on. The prisoner is brought into court. He looks at the judge in his robes of office; and sees he is the despised friend who came to him in his cell. But now his countenance is solemn and his voice severe. He who was refused as a friend now appears only as a judge.

Sinner, he who as a judge will occupy the throne at the last day, comes to you in your prison, and offers to be your Savior. He is willing to plead your cause, and promises you a free and full deliverance at the trial. Do not refuse him, for soon you must stand at his bar. Trust in him as your Advocate, if you would not tremble before him as your judge. Accept his invitation, so you will never have to hear him pronounce your doom. Welcome him now to your heart, so that he may welcome you then to his kingdom.

Matthew 25:31-46 "When the Son of Man comes in his glory, and all the angels with him, then he will sit on his glorious throne. Before him will be gathered all the nations, and he will separate people one from another as a shepherd separates the sheep from the goats. And he will place the sheep on his right, but the goats on the left. Then the King will say to those on his right, 'Come, you who are blessed by my Father, inherit the kingdom prepared for you from the foundation of the world. For I was hungry and you gave me food, I was thirsty and you gave me drink, I was a stranger and you welcomed me, I was

80

naked and you clothed me, I was sick and you visited me, I was in prison and you came to me.' Then the righteous will answer him, saying, 'Lord, when did we see you hungry and feed you, or thirsty and give you drink? And when did we see you a stranger and welcome you, or naked and clothe you? And when did we see you sick or in prison and visit you?' And the King will answer them, 'Truly, I say to you, as you did it to one of the least of these my brothers, you did it to me.' "Then he will say to those on his left, 'Depart from me, you cursed, into the eternal fire prepared for the devil and his angels. For I was hungry and you gave me no food, I was thirsty and you gave me no drink, I was a stranger and you did not welcome me, naked and you did not clothe me, sick and in prison and you did not visit me.' Then they also will answer, saying, 'Lord, when did we see you hungry or thirsty or a stranger or naked or sick or in prison, and did not minister to you?' Then he will answer them, saying, 'Truly, I say to you, as you did not do it to one of the least of these, you did not do it to me.' And these will go away into eternal punishment, but the righteous into eternal life."

2 Corinthians 5:10 For we must all appear before the judgment seat of Christ, so that each one may receive what is due for what he has done in the body, whether good or evil.

1 Thessalonians 4:16-18 For the Lord himself will descend from heaven with a cry of command, with the voice of an archangel, and with the sound of the trumpet of God. And the dead in Christ will rise

first. Then we who are alive, who are left, will be caught up together with them in the clouds to meet the Lord in the air, and so we will always be with the Lord. Therefore encourage one another with these words.

Revelation 1:7 Behold, he is coming with the clouds, and every eye will see him, even those who pierced him, and all tribes of the earth will wail on account of him. Even so. Amen.

Chapter 15

WHERE IS JESUS

It was the language of Job, "O that I knew where I might find him, if only I could go to his dwelling!" Is this your language, poor sinner? Are you anxious to know where to find Jesus? He is no longer on earth in human form, but has returned to heaven. There you may find him, seated on a throne of mercy, waiting to give eternal life to all who come to him. You may think it far to go, but the prayers of sinners reach heaven the very moment they are uttered, and are listened to by Jesus with much attention. Yet if this seems hard to understand, know assuredly that Jesus is not only in heaven, but on earth, too. He is God, and therefore is everywhere.

He said to his disciples, "I am with you always." He is constantly present among us. In the sick room, Jesus is there, ready to comfort the afflicted disciple who lies on that bed of pain. In the secret spot to which the sinner has gone to confess his sins, there is Jesus waiting to say, "Be of good cheer; your sins are forgiven you: go in peace." In the church or the room where many or few have assembled to praise and pray, there is Jesus waiting to supply their wants. "Wherever two or three are gathered together in my name, there am I in the middle of them."

Reader, he is near you. Now, while your eye reads this page, he stands close at your side. He whispers in your ear. He invites you to seek him. If you are anxious to find him, you have no long journey to take, no long time to wait before your request can reach his ear. He is nearer than the friend sitting beside you, for he is at your heart's door, knocking for entrance. Wherever you go he follows you, his hands loaded with blessings, which he offers to you freely. He is with you in your path, and when you are lying down; but it is always to do you good. In the morning he stands at your bedside, offering to clothe you with his white robe of righteousness; and when you are seated at the table, he asks you to eat that bread of life which will save your soul from death. He is so near that he will notice your first faint effort to come to him, and will stretch out his hand to help you. He is so near that he will see your first tear of repentance, and catch your first sigh for pardon. He is so near that before you call he will answer, and while you are still speaking he will hear. Sinner, wherever you are, there is Jesus. So that in all countries, under all circumstances, by day and by night, at home and abroad **you may come to Jesus**.

Psalm 139:1-24 O LORD, you have searched me and known me! You know when I sit down and when I rise up; you discern my thoughts from afar. You search out my path and my lying down and are acquainted with all my ways. Even before a word is on my tongue, behold, O LORD, you know it altogether. You hem me in, behind and before, and lay your hand upon me. Such knowledge is too wonderful for me; it is high; I cannot attain it. Where shall I go from your Spirit? Or where shall I flee from your presence? If I ascend to heaven, you are there! If I make my bed in Sheol, you are there! If I take the wings of the morning and dwell in the uttermost parts of the sea, even there your hand shall lead me, and your right hand shall hold me. If I say, "Surely the darkness shall cover me, and the light about me be night," even the darkness is not dark to you; the night is bright as the day, for darkness is as light with you.

For you formed my inward parts; you knitted me together in my mother's womb. I praise you, for I am fearfully and wonderfully made. Wonderful are your works; my soul knows it very well. My frame was not hidden from you, when I was being made in secret, intricately woven in the depths of the earth. Your eyes saw my unformed substance; in your book were written, every one of them, the days that were formed for me, when as yet there was none of them. How precious to me are your thoughts, O God! How vast is the sum of them! If I would count them, they are more than the sand. I awake, and I am still with you.

Oh that you would slay the wicked, O God! O men of blood, depart from me! They speak against you with malicious intent; your enemies take your name in vain. Do I not hate those who hate you, O LORD? And do I not loathe those who rise up against you? I hate them with complete hatred; I count them my enemies.

Search me, O God, and know my heart! Try me and know my thoughts! And see if there be any grievous way in me, and lead me in the way everlasting!

Isaiah 65:24 Before they call I will answer; while they are yet speaking I will hear.

Matthew 18:20 For where two or three are gathered in my name, there am I among them."

John 14:18-23 "I will not leave you as orphans; I will come to you. Yet a little while and the world will see me no more, but you will see me. Because I live, you also will live. In that day you will know that I am in my Father, and you in me, and I in you. Whoever has my commandments and keeps them, he it is who loves me. And he who loves me will be loved by my Father, and I will love him and manifest myself to him." Judas (not Iscariot) said to him, "Lord, how is it that you will manifest yourself to us, and not to the world?" Jesus answered him, "If anyone loves me, he will keep my word, and my Father will love him, and we will come to him and make our home with him.

Chapter 16

WHAT IS MEANT BY COMING TO JESUS

"Much is said of coming to Jesus, but how can I come? He is in heaven, and how can I go there to speak to him? I am told he is also everywhere, but I cannot see him, and how can I go to him? If he were but on earth as he once was, there is nothing I would not do in order to get to him. I would sell all I possess to pay for my journey; I would travel hundreds of miles. No difficulties would slow me. I would set off at once. I would go to him and push my way through the crowd, as the sick used to do, in order to be healed. I would fall down before him, and lay hold of his garment, or embrace his feet; and I would say, 'Lord Jesus, save me. I came not to be healed of blindness or lameness, or leprosy, but of sin. My heart is diseased with wickedness. I am in danger of God's wrath, and of eternal damnation. Lord, save me, or I perish.' But alas, Jesus is no longer among us, and I cannot understand what is meant by coming to him."

Dear reader, do all this in your heart, and then you will come to Jesus. What do you think would be the advantage of going to him, and falling before him, and holding his garment, and speaking to him as the sick and the lame used to do? Would it not be to let him know your wants? These he knows already. Without all this trouble, you can make him understand that you wish him to save you. Think of him, let your heart feel respect for him, and let your cries ascend to him, just as if you saw him. Be as earnest as if there was a crowd round him which you wished to push through. Call to him as that blind man did, who, though he did not see him, cried out, "Jesus, son of David, have mercy on me!"

You are better off than they who lived when he dwelt on earth. They had often to journey far. They sometimes could not get near him for the mass of people. But you may have him as much to yourself as if there were no other sinner that needed him. He is always near and within call; and though you cannot see him, he sees you, knows all you feel, and hears all you say. Coming to Jesus is the desire of the heart after him. It is to feel our sin and misery; to believe that he is able and willing to pardon, comfort, and save us; to ask him to help us, and to trust in him as our Friend. To have just the same feelings and desires as if he were visibly present, and we came and implored him to bless us, is to come to him, though we do not see his face nor hear his voice. Repenting sinner, your very desire for pardon, your prayer, "Jesus, save me"-- this is coming to him.

Chapter 17

COME BY PRAYER

Though you cannot see Jesus, you can speak to him. You can pray. God has permitted, and even commanded us to do this. How great a privilege to be allowed to speak to God. "Call upon me in the day of trouble." "Watch and pray." "Pray without ceasing." Prayer requires no fine, well-arranged sentences. The simplest utterance of your heart's desire is prayer. Those desires, themselves, unbreathed, are prayer. You need not wait until you can enter a church to pray; you may pray everywhere.

And Jesus is always waiting for the prayers of poor sinners; so that not one ever escapes his notice. His ear is always open. It is difficult to speak to kings and princes: they can only be seen sometimes, and then only a few persons are permitted to come near them. But all may come with their petitions to Jesus, however poor and despised, and at all times, too. Whatever good things you want for the soul, pray. For pardon, for a new heart, for faith, for holiness, for comfort, pray. You cannot pray in vain. You may be sure of such prayers being answered. There are some things which even God cannot do. He cannot sin, and he cannot refuse to listen to a poor sinner's prayer, for he has promised. "Ask, and it shall be given you," said Jesus: and his word declares, "He cannot deny himself." Be then encouraged to pray. However vile and helpless you think you are, you are not too bad to pray. Pray, if you can only utter such a petition as this, "Save me, Lord, or I perish!"

Make a habit of prayer. Find some place where you can be alone. "When you pray, enter into the closet, and shut the door." Rise before the work of the day begins, that you may have time to pray. Lay open your heart before God. Tell him how vile, and helpless, and wretched you are. Confess your sins, and cry for pardon. Read the Bible, and ask for that holiness which is commended there. Say, "Lord, I am ignorant, teach me. My heart is hard, soften it. Convert me by your Holy Spirit. Help me to come to Jesus--to believe, love, and obey him. Save me from sin, and fit me for heaven!" And let your heart throughout the day often ascend to God, even while engaged in your necessary labor. "Pray without ceasing." If the answer does not seem to come at once, pray on, and success is certain. A praying soul can never be lost. You cannot perish while you are sincerely calling upon Jesus, saying, "Lord, have mercy upon me a sinner."

Psalm 55:17 Evening and morning and at noon I utter my complaint and moan, and he hears my voice.

Psalm 65:2 O you who hear prayer, to you shall all flesh come.

Psalm 102:17 he regards the prayer of the destitute and does not despise their prayer.

Matthew 6:5-6 "And when you pray, you must not be like the hypocrites. For they love to stand and pray in the synagogues and at the street corners, that they may be seen by others. Truly, I say to you, they have received their reward. But when you pray, go into your room and shut the door and pray to your Father who is in secret. And your Father who sees in secret will reward you.

Luke 18:1-14 And he told them a parable to the effect that they ought always to pray and not lose heart. He said, "In a certain city there was a judge who neither feared God nor respected man. And there was a widow in that city who kept coming to him and saying, 'Give me justice against my adversary.' For a while he refused, but afterward he said to himself, 'Though I neither fear God nor respect man, yet because this widow keeps bothering me, I will give her justice, so that she will not beat me down by her continual coming.'" And the Lord said, "Hear what the unrighteous judge says. And will not God give justice to his elect, who cry to him day and night? Will he delay long over them? I tell you, he will give justice to them speedily. Nevertheless, when the Son of Man comes, will he find faith on earth?"

He also told this parable to some who trusted in themselves that they were righteous, and treated others with contempt: "Two men went up into the temple to pray, one a Pharisee and the other a tax collector. The Pharisee, standing by himself, prayed thus: 'God, I thank you that I am not like other men, extortioners, unjust, adulterers, or even like this tax collector. I fast twice a week; I give tithes of all that I get.' But the tax collector, standing far off, would not even lift up his eyes to heaven, but beat his breast, saying, 'God, be merciful to me, a sinner!' I tell you, this man went down to his house justified, rather than the other. For everyone who exalts himself will be humbled, but the one who humbles himself will be exalted."

Acts 10:9 The next day, as they were on their journey and approaching the city, Peter went up on the housetop about the sixth hour to pray.

Philippians 4:6 do not be anxious about anything, but in everything by prayer and supplication with thanksgiving let your requests be made known to God.

1 Thessalonians 5:17 pray without ceasing,

Chapter 18

COME IN THE BOLDNESS OF PRAYER

It is wonderful that creatures so sinful as we are, should be allowed to pray at all. When we consider what we are, and what God is, we may well tremble when we come to him, and fear lest he should reject us. But he has encouraged us to come, even with "boldness, to the throne of grace." This does not mean that we are to come without deep reverence and humility, but that we are to pray with a full confidence that God will answer us.

There are many examples of answers to prayer. Hezekiah prayed, and the army of Sennacherib was struck with death. Elijah prayed, and fire came down to consume his sacrifice. The apostles prayed, and the Holy Spirit descended upon them with miraculous gifts. The church prayed, and Peter was delivered from prison by an angel. We are not to expect that all we ask for respecting this life will be given us, for we often desire what would do us harm. We may be sure, however, that God will give us what is best. But when we pray for blessings for our souls--for pardon, and holiness, and salvation--we may be quite certain of being answered; for we are told, that if we ask anything according to God's will, he hears us; and we are also told, that God is "willing that all men should be saved."

Jesus said, "Ask, and it shall be given;" and, "Whatever you shall ask in my name, that will I do." He prays for us. Our best prayers are far too unworthy for God to notice, but he listens because Jesus pleads. If you wrote a petition to a king, but none at the palace knew you, and you were dressed in rags, and after doing your best, the writing was covered with blots, would you not fear that you would never be admitted, or if you were, that the petition would not be read? But suppose the king's son were to come, and say, "I will present your petition myself, and ask my father to grant it." Jesus does this. He presents our feeble prayers, and says, "For my sake, bless this poor sinner, and grant his request." And we are told that "him the Father hears always." "He ever lives to make intercession."

Trembling, mourning sinner, rejoice. You have a friend at court. However unworthy your petitions are, Jesus prays for you, and his prayers always prevail. What more can you need to encourage you? Come then with "boldness to the throne of grace, that you may obtain mercy, and find grace to help in time of need."

1 Kings 18:21-39 And Elijah came near to all the people and said, "How long will you go limping between two different opinions? If the LORD is God, follow him; but if Baal, then follow him." And the people did not answer him a word. Then Elijah said to the people, "I, even I only, am left a prophet of the LORD, but Baal's prophets are 450 men. Let two bulls be given to us, and let them choose one bull for themselves and cut it in pieces and lay it on the wood, but put no fire to it. And I will prepare the other bull and lay it on the wood and put no fire to it. And you call upon the name of your god, and I will call

94

upon the name of the LORD, and the God who answers by fire, he is God." And all the people answered, "It is well spoken."

Then Elijah said to the prophets of Baal, "Choose for yourselves one bull and prepare it first, for you are many, and call upon the name of your god, but put no fire to it." And they took the bull that was given them, and they prepared it and called upon the name of Baal from morning until noon, saying, "O Baal, answer us!" But there was no voice, and no one answered. And they limped around the altar that they had made. And at noon Elijah mocked them, saying, "Cry aloud, for he is a god. Either he is musing, or he is relieving himself, or he is on a journey, or perhaps he is asleep and must be awakened." And they cried aloud and cut themselves after their custom with swords and lances, until the blood gushed out upon them. And as midday passed, they raved on until the time of the offering of the oblation, but there was no voice. No one answered; no one paid attention.

Then Elijah said to all the people, "Come near to me." And all the people came near to him. And he repaired the altar of the LORD that had been thrown down. Elijah took twelve stones, according to the number of the tribes of the sons of Jacob, to whom the word of the LORD came, saying, "Israel shall be your name," and with the stones he built an altar in the name of the LORD. And he made a trench about the altar, as great as would contain two {measures} of seed. And he put the wood in order and cut the bull in pieces and laid it on the wood. And he said, "Fill four jars with water and pour it on the burnt offering and on the wood." And he said, "Do it a second time." And they did it a second time. And he said, "Do it a third time." And they

95

did it a third time. And the water ran around the altar and filled the trench also with water. And at the time of the offering of the oblation, Elijah the prophet came near and said, "O LORD, God of Abraham, Isaac, and Israel, let it be known this day that you are God in Israel, and that I am your servant, and that I have done all these things at your word. Answer me, O LORD, answer me, that this people may know that you, O LORD, are God, and that you have turned their hearts back." Then the fire of the LORD fell and consumed the burnt offering and the wood and the stones and the dust, and licked up the water that was in the trench. And when all the people saw it, they fell on their faces and said, "The LORD, he is God; the LORD, he is God."

Matthew 7:7-11 "Ask, and it will be given to you; seek, and you will find; knock, and it will be opened to you. For everyone who asks receives, and the one who seeks finds, and to the one who knocks it will be opened.

Or which one of you, if his son asks him for bread, will give him a stone? Or if he asks for a fish, will give him a serpent? If you then, who are evil, know how to give good gifts to your children, how much more will your Father who is in heaven give good things to those who ask him!

John 14:13-14 Whatever you ask in my name, this I will do, that the Father may be glorified in the Son. If you ask me anything in my name, I will do it.

Acts 12:5-17 So Peter was kept in prison, but earnest prayer for him was made to God by the church.

Now when Herod was about to bring him out, on that very night, Peter was sleeping between two soldiers, bound with two chains, and sentries before the door were guarding the prison. And behold, an angel of the Lord stood next to him, and a light shone in the cell. He struck Peter on the side and woke him, saying, "Get up quickly." And the chains fell off his hands. And the angel said to him, "Dress yourself and put on your sandals." And he did so. And he said to him, "Wrap your cloak around you and follow me." And he went out and followed him. He did not know that what was being done by the angel was real, but thought he was seeing a vision. When they had passed the first and the second guard, they came to the iron gate leading into the city. It opened for them of its own accord, and they went out and went along one street, and immediately the angel left him.

When Peter came to himself, he said, "Now I am sure that the Lord has sent his angel and rescued me from the hand of Herod and from all that the Jewish people were expecting." When he realized this, he went to the house of Mary, the mother of John whose other name was Mark, where many were gathered together and were praying. And when he knocked at the door of the gateway, a servant girl named Rhoda came to answer. Recognizing Peter's voice, in her joy she did not open the gate but ran in and reported that Peter was standing at the gate. They said to her, "You are out of your mind." But she kept insisting that it was so, and they kept saying, "It is his angel!"

But Peter continued knocking, and when they opened, they saw him and were amazed. But motioning to them with his hand to be silent, he described to them how the Lord had brought him out of the prison. And he said, "Tell these things to James and to the brothers." Then he departed and went to another place.

Hebrews 4:14-16 Since then we have a great high priest who has passed through the heavens, Jesus, the Son of God, let us hold fast our confession. For we do not have a high priest who is unable to sympathize with our weaknesses, but one who in every respect has been tempted as we are, yet without sin. Let us then with confidence draw near to the throne of grace, that we may receive mercy and find grace to help in time of need.

Hebrews 7:25 Consequently, he is able to save to the uttermost those who draw near to God through him, since he always lives to make intercession for them.

1 John 5:14 And this is the confidence that we have toward him, that if we ask anything according to his will he hears us.

Chapter 19

COME IN FAITH

In the New Testament we read very much about faith. We are said to be "justified by faith," and "saved by faith," and are told to "believe in the Lord Jesus Christ, that we may be saved." Faith is confidence, reliance. If I am hungry, and a kind friend offers me something and says it is bread, but it is dark, and I cannot see, yet, if I begin at once to eat it, this is faith. I trust in his word. If I am sick, and medicine is given me which I am told will do me good, and I drink it, this is faith. I believe or have confidence in the doctor's skill.

Jesus came into the world to die for sinners. He says, "Believe in me. I have purchased a full pardon for you, and you may go free. It cost my own blood to obtain it, but you are freely welcome to it. If you will obey my words, and trust in my protection, I will engage to save you from death and hell: I am quite able to do this. Here is bread to eat, which will make you live for ever if you eat it; here is a medicine which will cure your soul's sickness that you shall never die. Come unto me--believe in me, and you shall be saved."

Faith is just trusting to what Jesus says. Faith is simply coming to Jesus. He has died for you. Believe it, and take the benefit of his dying. He has opened the prison door for you. Believe it, and make your escape. He is willing to bear your burden for you. Believe it, and cast your sins upon him. He has paid all your debts. Rejoice. He brings

ation to you, and says, "It shall be yours, if you are willing." Stretch forth your hand, take it with a grateful heart. Like the prodigal in the parable, you have wandered far from home; but Jesus has obtained for you permission to return. Your Father, for his sake, is willing to welcome you back. Believe it, and say, "I will get up and go to my Father."

You desire to be trusted by your husband, or wife, or children; you would feel hurt by their doubting your word. So Jesus wishes to be believed when he says, "Poor sinner, I am able and willing to save you. Come unto me." Do not grieve him by distrusting his word. If you do not come because you think you are too great a sinner, you say, in effect, that he is not able to save you, though he tells us, "he is able to save to the uttermost ALL who come." You make him a liar. Believe that he really will do what he promises. Go to him at once. Say to him, "Lord, I believe; help my unbelief. you are able to save to the uttermost--save me."

John 3:14-36 And as Moses lifted up the serpent in the wilderness, so must the Son of Man be lifted up, that whoever believes in him may have eternal life.

"For God so loved the world, that he gave his only Son, that whoever believes in him should not perish but have eternal life. For God did not send his Son into the world to condemn the world, but in order that the world might be saved through him.

Whoever believes in him is not condemned, but whoever does not believe is condemned already, because he has not believed in the name

100

of the only Son of God. And this is the judgment: the light has come into the world, and people loved the darkness rather than the light because their works were evil. For everyone who does wicked things hates the light and does not come to the light, lest his works should be exposed. But whoever does what is true comes to the light, so that it may be clearly seen that his works have been carried out in God."

After this Jesus and his disciples went into the Judean countryside, and he remained there with them and was baptizing. John also was baptizing at Aenon near Salim, because water was plentiful there, and people were coming and being baptized (for John had not yet been put in prison).

Now a discussion arose between some of John's disciples and a Jew over purification. And they came to John and said to him, "Rabbi, he who was with you across the Jordan, to whom you bore witness— look, he is baptizing, and all are going to him." John answered, "A person cannot receive even one thing unless it is given him from heaven. You yourselves bear me witness, that I said, 'I am not the Christ, but I have been sent before him.' The one who has the bride is the bridegroom. The friend of the bridegroom, who stands and hears him, rejoices greatly at the bridegroom's voice. Therefore this joy of mine is now complete. He must increase, but I must decrease."

He who comes from above is above all. He who is of the earth belongs to the earth and speaks in an earthly way. He who comes from heaven is above all. He bears witness to what he has seen and heard, yet no one receives his testimony. Whoever receives his testimony sets his seal to this, that God is true. For he whom God has sent utters the words of God, for he gives the Spirit without measure. The Father loves the Son and has given all things into his hand. Whoever believes in the Son has eternal life; whoever does not obey the Son shall not see life, but the wrath of God remains on him.

Acts 16:30-31 Then he brought them out and said, "Sirs, what must I do to be saved?" And they said, "Believe in the Lord Jesus, and you will be saved, you and your household."

Romans 5:1 Therefore, since we have been justified by faith, we have peace with God through our Lord Jesus Christ.

Hebrews 11:1-40 Now faith is the assurance of things hoped for, the conviction of things not seen.

For by it the people of old received their commendation.

By faith we understand that the universe was created by the word of God, so that what is seen was not made out of things that are visible. By faith Abel offered to God a more acceptable sacrifice than Cain, through which he was commended as righteous, God commending him by accepting his gifts. And through his faith, though he died, he still speaks.

By faith Enoch was taken up so that he should not see death, and he was not found, because God had taken him. Now before he was taken he was commended as having pleased God. And without faith it is impossible to please him, for whoever would draw near to God must believe that he exists and that he rewards those who seek him.

By faith Noah, being warned by God concerning events as yet unseen, in reverent fear constructed an ark for the saving of his household. By this he condemned the world and became an heir of the righteousness that comes by faith.

By faith Abraham obeyed when he was called to go out to a place that he was to receive as an inheritance. And he went out, not knowing where he was going. By faith he went to live in the land of promise, as in a foreign land, living in tents with Isaac and Jacob, heirs with him of the same promise. For he was looking forward to the city that has foundations, whose designer and builder is God.

By faith Sarah herself received power to conceive, even when she was past the age, since she considered him faithful who had promised. Therefore from one man, and him as good as dead, were born descendants as many as the stars of heaven and as many as the innumerable grains of sand by the seashore.

These all died in faith, not having received the things promised, but having seen them and greeted them from afar, and having acknowledged that they were strangers and exiles on the earth. For people who speak thus make it clear that they are seeking a homeland. If they had been thinking of that land from which they had gone out, they would have had opportunity to return. But as it is, they desire a better country, that is, a heavenly one. Therefore God is not ashamed to be called their God, for he has prepared for them a city.

By faith Abraham, when he was tested, offered up Isaac, and he who had received the promises was in the act of offering up his only son, of whom it was said, "Through Isaac shall your offspring be named." He considered that God was able even to raise him from the dead, from which, figuratively speaking, he did receive him back.

By faith Isaac invoked future blessings on Jacob and Esau. By faith Jacob, when dying, blessed each of the sons of Joseph, bowing in worship over the head of his staff. By faith Joseph, at the end of his life, made mention of the exodus of the Israelites and gave directions concerning his bones.

By faith Moses, when he was born, was hidden for three months by his parents, because they saw that the child was beautiful, and they were not afraid of the king's edict. By faith Moses, when he was grown up, refused to be called the son of Pharaoh's daughter, choosing rather to be mistreated with the people of God than to enjoy the fleeting pleasures of sin. He considered the reproach of Christ greater wealth than the treasures of Egypt, for he was looking to the reward. By faith he left Egypt, not being afraid of the anger of the king, for he endured as seeing him who is invisible.

By faith he kept the Passover and sprinkled the blood, so that the Destroyer of the firstborn might not touch them. By faith the people crossed the Red Sea as on dry land, but the Egyptians, when they attempted to do the same, were drowned.

By faith the walls of Jericho fell down after they had been encircled for seven days. By faith Rahab the prostitute did not perish with those who were disobedient, because she had given a friendly welcome to the spies.

And what more shall I say? For time would fail me to tell of Gideon, Barak, Samson, Jephthah, of David and Samuel and the prophets—who through faith conquered kingdoms, enforced justice, obtained promises, stopped the mouths of lions, quenched the power of fire, escaped the edge of the sword, were made strong out of weakness, became mighty in war, put foreign armies to flight. Women received back their dead by resurrection. Some were tortured, refusing to accept release, so that they might rise again to a better life. Others suffered mocking and flogging, and even chains and imprisonment. They were stoned, they were sawn in two, they were killed with the sword. They went about in skins of sheep and goats, destitute, afflicted, mistreated —of whom the world was not worthy—wandering about in deserts and mountains, and in dens and caves of the earth. And all these, though commended through their faith, did not receive what was promised, since God had provided something better for us, that apart from us they should not be made perfect.

Chapter 20

COME AS A SINNER--JUST AS YOU ARE

Perhaps you say, "How can I, who am so vile a sinner, venture to come near the holy Jesus? Will he permit such a wretch to approach him? Must I not wait till I am more fit?"

Dear fellow-sinner, your very sinfulness is your best fitness. What you think to be a hinderance is your best encouragement; for, "Jesus Christ came into the world to save sinners," and therefore to save such as you. "I came not to call the righteous, but sinners to repentance." Not that there are any who are really righteous, but there are many who think that they are, and such persons will never be received by Christ. We must come to him in our true character, if we come at all. We are great sinners. We have broken God's laws. We have indulged in wickedness in our hearts, as well as in open conduct; we have quenched the Spirit, and despised the love of Jesus. Everything we do is full of imperfection. We cannot make ourselves pure. And if we come to Jesus pretending we are righteous, we only mock him. Instead of thinking we are "rich, and increased in goods, and have need of nothing," we must come as those who are "poor, and miserable, and blind, and naked." Thus we must come to Jesus, and confess our unworthiness.

In one of his parables he spoke of a self-righteous man, who thanked God that he was better than others; and of a broken-hearted penitent, who did not venture to raise his eyes to heaven, but beat upon his breast, saying, "God be merciful to me a sinner!" It was the latter who went home pardoned and saved. And if we would be accepted by Jesus, we must go to him in the same spirit, saying, "God be merciful to me a sinner!" And we must not wait, thinking that we shall ever be more worthy. No, our souls are stained through and through with sin, and all our washing will never get rid of one dark spot. The blood of Christ alone can make us clean. We can never make ourselves better. We must come to Jesus to make us better; and till then nothing is done. Our very first duty is to come to Jesus.

Come then, poor sinner. Do not wait another moment, foolishly thinking you will be more fit by and by. You will never be more fit, and never more welcome, than at this moment. Jesus knows, far better than even you do, how sinful and vile you are; yet he does not say, "Wait," but "Come." Come then, with all your sins and weakness, and hardness of heart, come to Jesus. Come as a sinner, and come just as you are.

Psalm 51:1-19 Have mercy on me, O God, according to your steadfast love; according to your abundant mercy blot out my transgressions.

Wash me thoroughly from my iniquity, and cleanse me from my sin! For I know my transgressions, and my sin is ever before me. Against you, you only, have I sinned and done what is evil in your sight, so that you may be justified in your words and blameless in your judgment.

Behold, I was brought forth in iniquity, and in sin did my mother conceive me. Behold, you delight in truth in the inward being, and you teach me wisdom in the secret heart. Purge me with hyssop, and I shall be clean; wash me, and I shall be whiter than snow. Let me hear joy and gladness; let the bones that you have broken rejoice. Hide your face from my sins, and blot out all my iniquities.

Create in me a clean heart, O God, and renew a right spirit within me. Cast me not away from your presence, and take not your Holy Spirit from me. Restore to me the joy of your salvation, and uphold me with a willing spirit.

Then I will teach transgressors your ways, and sinners will return to you. Deliver me from bloodguiltiness, O God, O God of my salvation, and my tongue will sing aloud of your righteousness. O Lord, open my lips, and my mouth will declare your praise. For you will not delight in sacrifice, or I would give it; you will not be pleased with a burnt offering. The sacrifices of God are a broken spirit; a broken and contrite heart, O God, you will not despise. Do good to Zion in your good pleasure; build up the walls of Jerusalem; then will you delight in right sacrifices, in burnt offerings and whole burnt offerings; then bulls will be offered on your altar.

Matthew 9:10-13 And as Jesus reclined at table in the house, behold, many tax collectors and sinners came and were reclining with Jesus and his disciples. And when the Pharisees saw this, they said to his disciples, "Why does your teacher eat with tax collectors and sinners?" But when he heard it, he said, "Those who are well have no need of a physician, but those who are sick. Go and learn what this means, 'I desire mercy, and not sacrifice.' For I came not to call the righteous, but sinners."

Luke 18:9-14 He also told this parable to some who trusted in themselves that they were righteous, and treated others with contempt: "Two men went up into the temple to pray, one a Pharisee and the other a tax collector. The Pharisee, standing by himself, prayed thus: 'God, I thank you that I am not like other men, extortioners, unjust, adulterers, or even like this tax collector. I fast twice a week; I give tithes of all that I get.' But the tax collector, standing far off, would not even lift up his eyes to heaven, but beat his breast, saying, 'God, be merciful to me, a sinner!' I tell you, this man went down to his house justified, rather than the other. For everyone who exalts himself will be humbled, but the one who humbles himself will be exalted."

1 Timothy 1:15 The saying is trustworthy and deserving of full acceptance, that Christ Jesus came into the world to save sinners, of whom I am the foremost.

Revelation 3:17-18 For you say, I am rich, I have prospered, and I need nothing, not realizing that you are wretched, pitiable, poor, blind, and naked. I counsel you to buy from me gold refined by fire, so that you may be rich, and white garments so that you may clothe yourself and the shame of your nakedness may not be seen, and salve to anoint your eyes, so that you may see.

Chapter 21

BUT I AM NOT WORTHY, AND CANNOT COME CORRECTLY

If you imagine that any sinner is worthy of salvation, you quite mistake the nature of the gospel. It is a free gift, not a reward. No one is worthy. Paul, Peter, John were not worthy. But Jesus is so full of love that, unworthy as we all are, he invites us to come. If he makes our sin no objection, why should we? Jesus knows that filthy rags cover you, that a nauseous disease infects you; yet he says, "Come unto me." On account of these very things, he says, Come. How unreasonable, then, for you to refuse because you are unworthy. You might as well say you were too hungry to eat, or too poor to receive help, as that you are too unworthy to come for pardon. Your very unworthiness makes you welcome. But you say you cannot come as you ought. Then come as you can. Jesus did not say, "Come unto me running or walking upright," but simply, "Come." Come in any manner, and you will be received. **Come creeping, crawling--any way--only come**.

You say you do not repent enough. You never will; for penitence, like all other graces, is ever growing, and no one's penitence can equal his sins. But we are not saved because we repent enough, but, if we do repent at all, we are saved because Jesus died. You say you don't have enough love. You never will have, till you get to heaven. But we are saved, not because we love God, but **because he loves us**. You say you don't have enough faith. True, and every Christian needs to pray, "Lord, increase my faith." But if you truly look to Jesus for salvation, this is faith; and though very weak, none who possess it can perish. But perhaps you say you heart is totally hard, and therefore that your mere cries of distress are not prayers which God can accept. Be encouraged by the case of Simon Magus. "His heart was not right in the sight of God;" he was "in the gall of bitterness, and in the bond of iniquity;" yet Peter said, "If you indeed pray to God, your sins will be forgiven." Your condition cannot be worse than his; yet he was encouraged to come to Jesus. Come with a broken heart, he may heal it; or as Leighton says, "If you find it unbroken, yet give it to him, with a desire that it may be broken."

However unable to come aright, make the effort: come as you can, only come; and Jesus will not, cannot reject you.

Acts 2:22-23 "Men of Israel, hear these words: Jesus of Nazareth, a man attested to you by God with mighty works and wonders and signs that God did through him in your midst, as you yourselves know—this Jesus, delivered up according to the definite plan and foreknowledge of God, you crucified and killed by the hands of lawless men.

Acts 2:36-42 Let all the house of Israel therefore know for certain that God has made him both Lord and Christ, this Jesus whom you crucified."

Now when they heard this they were cut to the heart, and said to Peter and the rest of the apostles, "Brothers, what shall we do?" And

Peter said to them, "Repent and be baptized every one of you in the name of Jesus Christ for the forgiveness of your sins, and you will receive the gift of the Holy Spirit. For the promise is for you and for your children and for all who are far off, everyone whom the Lord our God calls to himself." And with many other words he bore witness and continued to exhort them, saying, "Save yourselves from this crooked generation." So those who received his word were baptized, and there were added that day about three thousand souls. And they devoted themselves to the apostles' teaching and the fellowship, to the breaking of bread and the prayers.

Acts 3:13-19 The God of Abraham, the God of Isaac, and the God of Jacob, the God of our fathers, glorified his servant Jesus, whom you delivered over and denied in the presence of Pilate, when he had decided to release him. But you denied the Holy and Righteous One, and asked for a murderer to be granted to you, and you killed the Author of life, whom God raised from the dead. To this we are witnesses. And his name—by faith in his name—has made this man strong whom you see and know, and the faith that is through Jesus has given the man this perfect health in the presence of you all. And now, brothers, I know that you acted in ignorance, as did also your rulers. But what God foretold by the mouth of all the prophets, that his Christ would suffer, he thus fulfilled. Repent therefore, and turn back, that your sins may be blotted out,

Acts 3:26 God, having raised up his servant, sent him to you first, to bless you by turning every one of you from your wickedness.

Acts 8:18-23 Now when Simon saw that the Spirit was given through the laying on of the apostles' hands, he offered them money, saying, "Give me this power also, so that anyone on whom I lay my hands may receive the Holy Spirit." But Peter said to him, "May your silver perish with you, because you thought you could obtain the gift of God with money! You have neither part nor lot in this matter, for your heart is not right before God. Repent, therefore, of this wickedness of yours, and pray to the Lord that, if possible, the intent of your heart may be forgiven you. For I see that you are in the gall of bitterness and in the bond of iniquity."

Revelation 22:17 The Spirit and the Bride say, "Come." And let the one who hears say, "Come." And let the one who is thirsty come; let the one who desires take the water of life without price.

Chapter 22

BUT I FEAR I AM NOT ONE OF THE ELECT

You have no cause for this fear but your own imagination. Has God, or an angel, or the Bible told you so? Election, whatever it means, is God's work, not yours. Do not perplex yourself with his secret counsels, but attend to your own plain duties. "The secret things belong to the LORD our God, but the things that are revealed belong to us and to our children forever, that we may do all the words of this law." We must leave the secret things, and concentrate on the revealed. Our duty is to do according to God's law. And this law is most clear. You are nowhere told you are not elect; but you are told that Jesus died for you, and you are invited to come to him.

Irritate your mind, then, no longer about such difficult subjects as election, but promptly obey what God commands. He says,"Cast away from you all the transgressions that you have committed, and make yourselves a new heart and a new spirit. Turn from your evil ways. Repent, and believe the gospel. Believe in the Lord Jesus Christ, and you shall be saved. Ask, and it shall be given you; seek, and you shall find; knock, and it shall be opened. Draw near to God, and he will draw near to you. Whoever comes to me I will never cast out." Do what God says, and your salvation will be sure.

Suppose you were very poor, and a rich man were to announce that he would give a sum of money to a hundred persons whose names no one knew but himself, but at the same time promised that he would give it to every one who applied for it; would you say, "I am afraid I am not among the favored number, therefore I will not ask for the money?" No; you would rather say, "Whether I am among the hundred or not, every one is invited, and therefore I will go." Do the same respecting eternal life. Do not sit still, teasing yourself with useless inquiries whether your name is in God's book.

Are you a sinner? "Oh yes." Well, then you are invited; for "Jesus came to save sinners," and "he is the propitiation for the sins of the whole world." The invitation is universal. "Let the one who desires take the water of life without price." Jesus did not say, "Come unto me, you whose names are in the book of life," but, "Come unto me, all you that labor and are heavy laden." Are you heavy laden with sin? Then come to Jesus and your salvation is certain. Come to Jesus, and then you may be sure your name will be found in the book of life. Come to Jesus, and you will be received as one of the elect; but if you stay away, you will perish.

Deuteronomy 29:29 "The secret things belong to the LORD our God, but the things that are revealed belong to us and to our children forever, that we may do all the words of this law.

Ezekial 18:31 Cast away from you all the transgressions that you have committed, and make yourselves a new heart and a new spirit! Why will you die, O house of Israel?

Joel 2:12-13 "Yet even now," declares the LORD, "return to me with all your heart, with fasting, with weeping, and with mourning; and rend your hearts and not your garments." Return to the LORD your God, for he is gracious and merciful, slow to anger, and abounding in steadfast love; and he relents over disaster.

Mark 1:15 and saying, "The time is fulfilled, and the kingdom of God is at hand; repent and believe in the gospel."

1 John 2:2 He is the propitiation for our sins, and not for ours only but also for the sins of the whole world.

Chapter 23

BUT I HAVE NO FAITH

"I do not feel my sins are forgiven, and I am not sure I am saved. Many say they know the time when they found salvation, and that they have an inward witness that all is right with them. They have found peace; but I have not. I am full of doubts and fears, have no faith, and therefore fear Jesus will never receive me."

My friend, you confound two things which greatly differ, faith and assurance. You have been speaking of assurance, not of faith. It is very delightful to feel sure of pardon and heaven; but it is quite possible not to feel this, and yet to possess faith. Faith is coming to Jesus as a poor sinner, and trusting to him alone for salvation. Assurance is feeling certain we are saved. They are quite different things. Faith is necessary for salvation, but assurance is not. Many people possess an assurance which is false, while they are destitute of faith; and many also have true faith, but do not enjoy assurance.

Suppose you were shipwrecked, and clinging to a part of the vessel over which the waves were furiously breaking. A life-boat comes out to you. It is so well built that it cannot possibly sink. The rowers are so skillful that they never failed to bring it safe to shore. They invite you to enter. You know that the vessel you cling to will soon be dashed to pieces. You believe the boat will take you safe to shore. You enter it. But when the huge waves toss it up and down, and seem about to overwhelm it, you are afraid, and perhaps do not lose your fear till you reach the shore. Getting into the boat was faith--being afraid while in it was the lack of assurance. But though frightened, you were as safe as the rowers who had no fears. Your terrors did not endanger your safety, though it destroyed your peace.

We are in a storm. Our sins have raised up the winds and waves of divine justice. The law thunders as it curses against us. Hell yawns below. Jesus is like the life-boat. He comes out to us and invites us to forsake all our own refuges, which are as frail as a sinking wreck, and to cast ourselves on him. Trusting in him alone is faith, though when you think of your sins and infirmities you may be full of doubts and fears, and often think you are not safe. Take encouragement then, trembling sinner. Do you feel yourself lost without Jesus; and is it your earnest prayer, "Save, Lord, or I perish?" Then, whatever your gloomy doubts, you do possess faith, saving faith--that faith of which Paul spoke when he said, "Believe in the Lord Jesus Christ, and you will be saved." None can perish who come to Jesus in this manner.

Chapter 24

YOU WHO ARE YOUNG, COME

Youthful reader, be persuaded to give your early years to God. There is a special promise for you: "Those that seek me early shall find me." Perhaps you think, "I am too young to be religious yet; let me enjoy the world a little; I have plenty of time before me." Too young to be religious? But you are not too young to sin, or too young to die, or too young to be cast into hell. You may not live to reach manhood, much less old age. Multitudes die as young as you. If you enter a burial-ground, how many of the graves are those of young people. Death may be even now preparing to strike you. Oh then come at once to Jesus.

You greatly err, if you think religion will make you gloomy. It alone can render you truly happy. Many young people have come to Jesus, who will all tell you that the pleasures of piety are far better than all the delights of sin and vanity. You will find that this is true, if you come to Jesus. Is it likely he will let his followers be less happy than the servants of the world?

Besides, how can you dare to live a day longer rejecting him? He commands us at once to believe and obey him. Every day we put off repentance we commit a fresh act of rebellion, and treasure up wrath against the day of wrath. You say you will repent when you are old. But we need the Spirit of God to help us to repent; and if you say,

"While I am young I will serve Satan, and not till I am near death will I turn to God," do you think God will give you his Holy Spirit at all? Is not this to quench the Spirit? Will you not become quite careless, and indisposed to repent? Very few are converted when old. If you do not come to Jesus when you are young, it is likely that you will not come at all. Habit will fasten strong chains around you, which will be harder to break every day. While you wait, Satan works. He is busy tying knots. You are his prisoner; and he is making the cords which bind you more and more secure. Whenever you sin he ties another knot. Every impression you smother, every hour you delay, adds a fresh knot. If you do not escape now, how can you expect to break loose when you are weaker, and your bonds stronger?

Oh then, "Remember now your Creator in the days of your youth." Come at once to Jesus, if you wish to come at all. He will be your guide amid the snares, your comfort amid the sorrows, your guardian amid the dangers of life. Lose not for one day the privilege of possessing such a friend. Say from this moment, "My Father, you are the guide of my youth, the guide of the rest of my life."

Proverbs 3:1-24 My son, do not forget my teaching, but let your heart keep my commandments, for length of days and years of life and peace they will add to you. Let not steadfast love and faithfulness forsake you; bind them around your neck; write them on the tablet of your heart. So you will find favor and good success in the sight of God and man.

Trust in the LORD with all your heart, and do not lean on your own understanding. In all your ways acknowledge him, and he will make straight your paths. Be not wise in your own eyes; fear the LORD, and turn away from evil. It will be healing to your flesh and refreshment to your bones. Honor the LORD with your wealth and with the firstfruits of all your produce; then your barns will be filled with plenty, and your vats will be bursting with wine. My son, do not despise the LORD's discipline or be weary of his reproof, for the LORD reproves him whom he loves, as a father the son in whom he delights.

Blessed is the one who finds wisdom, and the one who gets understanding, for the gain from her is better than gain from silver and her profit better than gold. She is more precious than jewels, and nothing you desire can compare with her. Long life is in her right hand; in her left hand are riches and honor. Her ways are ways of pleasantness, and all her paths are peace. She is a tree of life to those who lay hold of her; those who hold her fast are called blessed.

The LORD by wisdom founded the earth; by understanding he established the heavens; by his knowledge the deeps broke open, and the clouds drop down the dew.

My son, do not lose sight of these— keep sound wisdom and discretion, and they will be life for your soul and adornment for your neck. Then you will walk on your way securely, and your foot will not stumble. If you lie down, you will not be afraid; when you lie down, your sleep will be sweet.

Proverbs 4:1-27 Hear, O sons, a father's instruction, and be attentive, that you may gain insight, for I give you good precepts; do not forsake my teaching. When I was a son with my father, tender, the only one in the sight of my mother, he taught me and said to me, "Let your heart hold fast my words; keep my commandments, and live. Get wisdom; get insight; do not forget, and do not turn away from the words of my mouth. Do not forsake her, and she will keep you; love her, and she will guard you.

The beginning of wisdom is this: Get wisdom, and whatever you get, get insight. Prize her highly, and she will exalt you; she will honor you if you embrace her. She will place on your head a graceful garland; she will bestow on you a beautiful crown."

Hear, my son, and accept my words, that the years of your life may be many. I have taught you the way of wisdom; I have led you in the paths of uprightness. When you walk, your step will not be hampered, and if you run, you will not stumble. Keep hold of instruction; do not let go; guard her, for she is your life. Do not enter the path of the wicked, and do not walk in the way of the evil. Avoid it; do not go on it; turn away from it and pass on. For they cannot sleep unless they have done wrong; they are robbed of sleep unless they have made someone stumble. For they eat the bread of wickedness and drink the wine of violence. But the path of the righteous is like the light of dawn, which shines brighter and brighter until full day. The way of the wicked is like deep darkness; they do not know over what they stumble.

My son, be attentive to my words; incline your ear to my sayings. Let them not escape from your sight; keep them within your heart. For they are life to those who find them, and healing to all their flesh. Keep your heart with all vigilance, for from it flow the springs of life. Put away from you crooked speech, and put devious talk far from you. Let your eyes look directly forward, and your gaze be straight before you. Ponder the path of your feet; then all your ways will be sure. Do not swerve to the right or to the left; turn your foot away from evil.

Proverbs 8:17 I love those who love me, and those who seek me diligently find me.

Ecclesiastes 12:1 Remember also your Creator in the days of your youth, before the evil days come and the years draw near of which you will say, "I have no pleasure in them"

Chapter 25

YOU WHO ARE ADVANCING IN YEARS, COME

With you the morning of life is over. You have reached the mountain top, or are traveling down the valley on the other side. You are rapidly drawing nearer the tomb. Perhaps you are still busily occupied in the necessary labors of life; or inclination and the love of gain may involve you in many engrossing cares. But do not forget the "one thing required." We can do without any thing else, even life itself; but we cannot do without Jesus. The salvation of the soul is the one thing absolutely necessary. You have been busy for many years in the concerns of this life, but as yet have found no time for religion. Your chief business is not even begun. But what trifles are all things else in comparison. **In a few years it will be of no consequence whether we were rich or poor; but it will be of infinite consequence whether we come to Jesus or not.** Multitudes have died around you. Neighbors and friends, many with whom you were at school, or started in life, are in their graves. You have been spared. But you might have been cut down as a barren tree--unprepared. God's forbearance may be almost spent. Soon the sentence may be pronounced, "Cut it down; why obstruct the ground?"

Perhaps you are advanced in years. My aged friend, how many solemn warnings did you ignore? Your wrinkled features, white hair, decaying strength, loudly tell you that the end is near. You are tottering on the edge of the grave. The young may live many years, but you cannot. Soon, very soon, you must die. Oh, how dreadful to stand before the judgment-seat of Christ, and give an account of a long life spent in rejecting him--of thousands of Sabbaths and sermons and privileges neglected. O then come to Jesus now. Do not lose a moment. You don't have one to spare. You have indeed hardened your heart, and made repentance more difficult by neglecting religion so long; but if you earnestly implore the help of God's Holy Spirit, he will grant your petition even now. It is not too late. Even though you have refused to listen to him for so long, Jesus has not ceased to speak to you. Still he says, "Come unto me." He loves you still. He is waiting to save you still. Oh, do not trifle with him any longer. Look back. Death comes striding after you with rapid steps; he is very near. Judgment is close behind, and hell follows. They are on the point of seizing you. Flee this moment to Christ. Come to Jesus. He alone can save.

Matthew 6:19-24 "Do not lay up for yourselves treasures on earth, where moth and rust destroy and where thieves break in and steal, but lay up for yourselves treasures in heaven, where neither moth nor rust destroys and where thieves do not break in and steal. For where your treasure is, there your heart will be also.

"The eye is the lamp of the body. So, if your eye is healthy, your whole body will be full of light, but if your eye is bad, your whole body will be full of darkness. If then the light in you is darkness, how great is the darkness!

"No one can serve two masters, for either he will hate the one and love the other, or he will be devoted to the one and despise the other. You cannot serve God and money.

Luke 10:40-42 But Martha was distracted with much serving. And she went up to him and said, "Lord, do you not care that my sister has left me to serve alone? Tell her then to help me." But the Lord answered her, "Martha, Martha, you are anxious and troubled about many things, but one thing is necessary. Mary has chosen the good portion, which will not be taken away from her."

Luke 13:6-9 And he told this parable: "A man had a fig tree planted in his vineyard, and he came seeking fruit on it and found none. And he said to the vinedresser, 'Look, for three years now I have come seeking fruit on this fig tree, and I find none. Cut it down. Why should it use up the ground?' And he answered him, 'Sir, let it alone this year also, until I dig around it and put on manure. Then if it should bear fruit next year, well and good; but if not, you can cut it down.'"

Chapter 26

BACKSLIDER, COME

Yours is a peculiar case; for you have already come to Jesus, but have wandered from him. You have been near, but now you are afar off. Your sin is very great. You have experienced something of the love of Christ, yet have forsaken him. You have enjoyed clearer light and greater advantages than those who have never known what religion is. You have been admitted within the fold, and tasted the sweet pasture with which the good Shepherd feeds his flock, yet you have strayed from the sacred enclosure.

Your decline began perhaps in secret, by restraining prayer, and neglecting God's word. Or you yielded to some temptation, but did not go to Christ for pardon, and so you became gradually careless. You may still maintain an outward profession of piety, but your heart is not right in the sight of God. Perhaps you have plunged into worldly dissipations, and are an example of the saying, "If any man love the world, the love of the Father is not in him." Perhaps even worse, you have fallen into open sin, and brought public disgrace on the name of Christian. You have lost all those opportunities of doing good which, had you not been a backslider, you would have improved. Thus you have robbed God.

You have discouraged other professors by your coldness and inconsistency, and been a hinderance to many who were inquiring,

"What must I do to be saved?" Instead of being a blessing to others, you have been a curse. And what is more you have grieved the Holy Spirit, have crucified the Son of God afresh, and put him to an open shame.

Yet Jesus, the kind Shepherd whose fold you have left, is willing to welcome you back. He seeks the sheep that have gone astray. He says, "O Israel return unto the Lord your God. Say unto him, Take away all iniquity, and receive us graciously. I will heal their backslidings, I will love them freely; for my anger is turned away. Return, you backsliding children, and I will heal your backsliding, for I am merciful. Only acknowledge your iniquity, that you have transgressed against the Lord your God. Turn, O backsliding children, says the Lord!" Consider these kind words. Ponder well the parable of the prodigal son. What greater encouragement can you need? Though you have wandered from Jesus, you may come to him again. He is as willing to receive you as at first. Stop, then, in your backward career. Return unto the Lord.

Psalm 119:176 I have gone astray like a lost sheep; seek your servant, for I do not forget your commandments.

Jeremiah 3:12-14 Go, and proclaim these words toward the north, and say, "'Return, faithless Israel, declares the LORD. I will not look on you in anger, for I am merciful, declares the LORD; I will not be angry forever. Only acknowledge your guilt, that you rebelled against the LORD your God and scattered your favors among foreigners under every green tree, and that you have not obeyed my voice, declares the LORD.

Return, O faithless children, declares the LORD; for I am your master; I will take you, one from a city and two from a family, and I will bring you to Zion.

Jeremiah 3:22 "Return, O faithless sons; I will heal your faithlessness." "Behold, we come to you, for you are the LORD our God.

Hosea 14:1-4 Return, O Israel, to the LORD your God, for you have stumbled because of your iniquity. Take with you words and return to the LORD; say to him, "Take away all iniquity; accept what is good, and we will pay with bulls the vows of our lips. Assyria shall not save us; we will not ride on horses; and we will say no more, 'Our God,' to the work of our hands. In you the orphan finds mercy." I will heal their apostasy; I will love them freely, for my anger has turned from them.

Luke 15:1-32 Now the tax collectors and sinners were all drawing near to hear him. And the Pharisees and the scribes grumbled, saying, "This man receives sinners and eats with them." So he told them this parable: "What man of you, having a hundred sheep, if he has lost one of them, does not leave the ninety-nine in the open country, and go after the one that is lost, until he finds it? And when he has found it, he lays it on his shoulders, rejoicing. And when he comes home, he calls together his friends and his neighbors, saying to them, 'Rejoice with me, for I have found my sheep that was lost.' Just so, I tell you, there will be more joy in heaven over one sinner who repents than over ninety-nine righteous persons who need no repentance.

"Or what woman, having ten silver coins, if she loses one coin, does not light a lamp and sweep the house and seek diligently until she finds it? And when she has found it, she calls together her friends and neighbors, saying, 'Rejoice with me, for I have found the coin that I had lost.' Just so, I tell you, there is joy before the angels of God over one sinner who repents."

And he said, "There was a man who had two sons. And the younger of them said to his father, 'Father, give me the share of property that is coming to me.' And he divided his property between them. Not many days later, the younger son gathered all he had and took a journey into a far country, and there he squandered his property in reckless living. And when he had spent everything, a severe famine arose in that country, and he began to be in need. So he went and hired himself out to one of the citizens of that country, who sent him into his fields to feed pigs. And he was longing to be fed with the pods that the pigs ate, and no one gave him anything. "But when he came to himself, he said, 'How many of my father's hired servants have more than enough bread, but I perish here with hunger! I will arise and go to my father, and I will say to him, "Father, I have sinned against heaven and before you. I am no longer worthy to be called your son. Treat me as one of your hired servants."' And he arose and came to his father. But while he was still a long way off, his father saw him and felt compassion, and ran and embraced him and kissed him. And the son said to him, 'Father, I have sinned against heaven and before you. I am no longer worthy to be called your son.' But the father said to his servants, 'Bring quickly the best robe, and put it on him, and put a ring on his hand, and shoes on his feet. And bring the fattened calf and kill it, and let us eat and celebrate. For this my son was dead, and is alive again; he was lost, and is found.' And they began to celebrate.

"Now his older son was in the field, and as he came and drew near to the house, he heard music and dancing. And he called one of the servants and asked what these things meant. And he said to him, 'Your brother has come, and your father has killed the fattened calf, because he has received him back safe and sound.' But he was angry and refused to go in. His father came out and entreated him, but he answered his father, 'Look, these many years I have served you, and I never disobeyed your command, yet you never gave me a young goat, that I might celebrate with my friends. But when this son of yours came, who has devoured your property with prostitutes, you killed the fattened calf for him!' And he said to him, 'Son, you are always with me, and all that is mine is yours. It was fitting to celebrate and be glad, for this your brother was dead, and is alive; he was lost, and is found.'"

Chapter 27

DESPAIRING SINNER, COME

Perhaps you say, "The mercy of God is for others, not for me. I have been too wicked. I have abused the greatest privileges, and stifled the strongest convictions. I have fought against God, and committed crimes I shudder to think of. There can be no pardon for me."

Listen, sinner: God says, "Though your sins be as scarlet, they shall be white as snow." "As I live, I have no pleasure in the death of the wicked, but that he turn and live. Turn you, turn you: for why will you die?" Listen, sinner: "The blood of Jesus Christ cleanses us from all sin." ALL sin, and therefore yours. Listen: "He is able to save to the uttermost ALL who come unto God by him." And therefore YOU. Listen: "Jesus Christ came into the world to save sinners, of whom I am CHIEF." He saves the chief of sinners, and therefore can save you. David, who had committed murder--Peter, who denied him--the thief on the cross--thousands who cried, "Crucify him"--Paul the persecutor--were all saved. And He who saved them is able to save you.

Do you fear that you have committed the unpardonable sin? Your anxiety is a sure proof you have not committed it. Whatever that sin is, it is certain that if any one were to commit it, he would never feel any true penitence for it. For the Bible in every page tells us, that all who repent shall be forgiven, that all who seek mercy shall find it; and

Jesus says, "Whoever comes to me I will never cast out," that is, on no account whatever. So that we may be quite sure that no penitent sinner who comes to Jesus for pardon, has committed sins which cannot be forgiven. God is bound by his promise and oath to "abundantly pardon" every sinner who comes to Jesus for salvation.

But still you may say, "I am a lost sinner." A brother of the celebrated Whitefield was at tea with Lady Huntington, who endeavored to cheer his despairing soul by speaking of the infinite mercy of Christ. "My lady," said he, "it is true; I see it clearly: but there is no mercy for me; I am a wretch entirely lost." "I am glad to hear it, glad at my heart that you are a lost man," was her reply. "What, my lady; glad that I am a lost man?" "Yes, Mr. Whitefield, truly glad, for Jesus Christ came into the world to save the lost." That word cheered his soul. He believed in Jesus, and soon after died in peace. Sinner, rejoice; Jesus came to save the lost--to save YOU.

Isaiah 1:18 "Come now, let us reason together, says the LORD: though your sins are like scarlet, they shall be as white as snow; though they are red like crimson, they shall become like wool.

Ezekiel 18:30-32 "Therefore I will judge you, O house of Israel, every one according to his ways, declares the Lord GOD. Repent and turn from all your transgressions, lest iniquity be your ruin. Cast away from you all the transgressions that you have committed, and make yourselves a new heart and a new spirit! Why will you die, O house of

Israel? For I have no pleasure in the death of anyone, declares the Lord GOD; so turn, and live."

Ezekiel 33:11 Say to them, As I live, declares the Lord GOD, I have no pleasure in the death of the wicked, but that the wicked turn from his way and live; turn back, turn back from your evil ways, for why will you die, O house of Israel?

Luke 19:10 For the Son of Man came to seek and to save the lost.

John 6:37 All that the Father gives me will come to me, and whoever comes to me I will never cast out.

1 Timothy 1:15 The saying is trustworthy and deserving of full acceptance, that Christ Jesus came into the world to save sinners, of whom I am the foremost.

Hebrews 7:25 Consequently, he is able to save to the uttermost those who draw near to God through him, since he always lives to make intercession for them.

1 John 1:7 But if we walk in the light, as he is in the light, we have fellowship with one another, and the blood of Jesus his Son cleanses us from all sin.

Chapter 28

CARELESS SINNER, COME

What, a rebel against God--hastening now towards death--doomed to hell--yet careless? Reader, are you one of those who are so busy with the trifles of this world as to pay no attention to the eternal realities of the next world? Listen to the startling question of Jesus. Ponder it. "What shall it profit a man, if he gain the whole world, and lose his own soul?"

Suppose you saw a crowd walking along a meadow, at the end of which was a terrific precipice. They pass on merrily, plucking flowers, till, as they reach the edge, one after another falls over, and is dashed to pieces. Would you not call to them, "Stop, stop! as you value your lives, turn back?" You are strolling onwards to a far more terrible fate. Yawning beneath you is the lake of fire--and do you still go forward? Jesus calls to you, "Turn, turn; why will you die?" But you do not see the danger. You feel happy, and hope it will be all right with you hereafter.

Have you never seen how smooth the stream is just before it leaps down the cataract? Such is your peace, soon to be broken by a fatal plunge into endless torment. Many poisons are pleasant to the taste, and soothe those who drink into sweet slumbers, but from these slumbers they never awake. You are guzzling Satan's cup of death. What you think is a pleasant drink is deadly poison; and your unconcern about religion is the sign of how dreadfully it is operating on your soul.

Beware, lest you wake up in the flames of hell. Before it is too late shake off this lethargy. Your house is on fire; the roof will soon fall in and crush you. But you sit at ease, amused with trifles, and neglecting every warning. Many cry "fire, fire--flee for your life." But you pay no attention to the alarm. Jesus offers himself as a refuge, but in vain.

Yet, though you regard it not, you are in danger. In danger you draw every breath. Danger is your traveling companion when you journey, and danger haunts your home. Danger hovers over you during the bustle of the day, and danger peeps between your curtains amid the silence of night. You may be prosperous, beloved, flattered, and at ease; but you are in danger. You may drown engaged in business, or by plunging deeper and deeper into worldly dissipation and sin; but you are in danger--in danger of wrath, death, hell.

Oh flee to Jesus. There only are we safe. Escape by the door of salvation, while it is still open; for it will soon be shut, and then you will knock in vain.

Ecclesiastes 11:9 Rejoice, O young man, in your youth, and let your heart cheer you in the days of your youth. Walk in the ways of your heart and the sight of your eyes. But know that for all these things God will bring you into judgment.

Ezekiel 3:17-19 "Son of man, I have made you a watchman for the house of Israel. Whenever you hear a word from my mouth, you shall give them warning from me. If I say to the wicked, 'You shall surely die,' and you give him no warning, nor speak to warn the wicked from his wicked way, in order to save his life, that wicked person shall die for his iniquity, but his blood I will require at your hand. But if you warn the wicked, and he does not turn from his wickedness, or from his wicked way, he shall die for his iniquity, but you will have delivered your soul.

Ezekiel 33:1-11 The word of the LORD came to me: "Son of man, speak to your people and say to them, If I bring the sword upon a land, and the people of the land take a man from among them, and make him their watchman, and if he sees the sword coming upon the land and blows the trumpet and warns the people, then if anyone who hears the sound of the trumpet does not take warning, and the sword comes and takes him away, his blood shall be upon his own head. He heard the sound of the trumpet and did not take warning; his blood shall be upon himself. But if he had taken warning, he would have saved his life. But if the watchman sees the sword coming and does not blow the trumpet, so that the people are not warned, and the sword comes and takes any one of them, that person is taken away in his iniquity, but his blood I will require at the watchman's hand.

"So you, son of man, I have made a watchman for the house of Israel. Whenever you hear a word from my mouth, you shall give them warning from me. If I say to the wicked, O wicked one, you shall surely die, and you do not speak to warn the wicked to turn from his way, that wicked person shall die in his iniquity, but his blood I will require at your hand. But if you warn the wicked to turn from his way, and he does not turn from his way, that person shall die in his iniquity, but you will have delivered your soul.

"And you, son of man, say to the house of Israel, Thus have you said: 'Surely our transgressions and our sins are upon us, and we rot away because of them. How then can we live?' Say to them, As I live, declares the Lord GOD, I have no pleasure in the death of the wicked, but that the wicked turn from his way and live; turn back, turn back from your evil ways, for why will you die, O house of Israel?

Mark 8:34-38 And calling the crowd to him with his disciples, he said to them, "If anyone would come after me, let him deny himself and take up his cross and follow me. For whoever would save his life will lose it, but whoever loses his life for my sake and the gospel's will save it. For what does it profit a man to gain the whole world and forfeit his soul? For what can a man give in return for his soul. For whoever is ashamed of me and of my words in this adulterous and sinful generation, of him will the Son of Man also be ashamed when he comes in the glory of his Father with the holy angels."

Luke 12:16-21 And he told them a parable, saying, "The land of a rich man produced plentifully, and he thought to himself, 'What shall I do, for I have nowhere to store my crops?' And he said, 'I will do this: I will tear down my barns and build larger ones, and there I will store all my grain and my goods. And I will say to my soul, "Soul, you have ample goods laid up for many years; relax, eat, drink, be merry."' But

God said to him, 'Fool! This night your soul is required of you, and the things you have prepared, whose will they be?' So is the one who lays up treasure for himself and is not rich toward God."

2 Peter 3:1-12 This is now the second letter that I am writing to you, beloved. In both of them I am stirring up your sincere mind by way of reminder, that you should remember the predictions of the holy prophets and the commandment of the Lord and Savior through your apostles.

Knowing this first of all, that scoffers will come in the last days with scoffing, following their own sinful desires. They will say, "Where is the promise of his coming? For ever since the fathers fell asleep, all things are continuing as they were from the beginning of creation."

For they deliberately overlook this fact, that the heavens existed long ago, and the earth was formed out of water and through water by the word of God, and that by means of these the world that then existed was deluged with water and perished. But by the same word the heavens and earth that now exist are stored up for fire, being kept until the day of judgment and destruction of the ungodly.

But do not overlook this one fact, beloved, that with the Lord one day is as a thousand years, and a thousand years as one day. The Lord is not slow to fulfill his promise as some count slowness, but is patient toward you, not wishing that any should perish, but that all should reach repentance.

But the day of the Lord will come like a thief, and then the heavens will pass away with a roar, and the heavenly bodies will be burned up and dissolved, and the earth and the works that are done on it will be exposed.

Since all these things are thus to be dissolved, what sort of people ought you to be in lives of holiness and godliness, waiting for and hastening the coming of the day of God, because of which the heavens will be set on fire and dissolved, and the heavenly bodies will melt as they burn!

Chapter 29

COME NOW: IT WILL BE HARDER WORK TOMORROW

Perhaps you think it will be as easy to repent at any future time as today. This is a most dangerous delusion. Impressions of all kinds wear away by repetition, unless they are made permanent by being acted upon. If you ever lived near a noisy mill, a roaring river, or the sea, you have found that the sound, which at first disturbed you, was afterwards scarcely noticed. Just so the truths of religion may deeply impress the mind; but if those impressions are not cherished, by acting in accordance with them, those truths will effect the mind less and less, till they are heard with total indifference. Jesus says, "Behold, I stand at the door and knock." He knocks by sermons, books, conversations, conscience, solemn warnings. The sound startles you; but if you do not rise and open the door, it will startle you less tomorrow, till at length you will not hear it at all. How many who once felt deeply about religion, now feel nothing, and are quickly and quietly traveling down to hell.

On the narrow ledges of the steep cliffs of the Yorkshire coast multitudes of sea fowl lay their eggs, by gathering which, some persons obtain a perilous livelihood. It once happened that a man, having fixed in the ground his iron bar, and having lowered himself down by the rope which was fastened to it, found, that, in consequence of the edge of the cliff bending over the part below, he could not reach the narrow ledge where the eggs were deposited, without swinging himself backwards and forwards. By this means he at last placed his foot on the rock, but in so doing lost his hold of the rope. His situation was most dreadful. The sea roared hundreds of feet below. It was impossible to climb either up or down. He must soon perish from want, or fall, and be dashed to pieces on the rocks. The rope was his only way of escape. It was still swinging to and fro; but when it settled it would be out of reach. Every time it approached him it was farther off than before. Every moment he waited his danger increased. He made up his mind. The next time the rope swung towards him he sprang forward, seized it, and reached the top in safety.

Sinner, your salvation is farther off every moment you wait. Hell is below. Death will soon cast you down. But Jesus is near to save you. He invites you to lay hold on him. It is your only hope. Grasp him by faith. You cannot miss your hold. He will hold you and draw you up to heaven. But the difficulty and danger are greater every moment you delay. Come to Jesus now.

Chapter 30

COME NOW: TOMORROW MAY BE TOO LATE

You have perhaps decided to come to Jesus, but not just now. Like Felix, you say, "Go away for the present. When I get an opportunity I will summon you." Satan knows that if you put religion off, he is likely to keep you captive forever. God says, "TODAY if you will hear my voice, harden not your hearts: behold NOW is the day of salvation." Satan whispers, "not today, but, tomorrow." He promises you shall give to God all your future days, if only he can secure for himself the present.

Oh, beware of tomorrow. Souls are generally lost, not because they resolve never to repent, but because they defer it till some future time, and still defer it till it is too late. Tomorrows have crowded hell. Perhaps you think you will wait till disease assails you. But a sick bed is the very worst place for repenting. Your mind may be so distracted by delirium, fever, or pain, or may so share in the weakness of the body, as to be unable to think. The peace in which multitudes seem to die is only the apathy of disease. Many, who, when ill, have professed to repent, on recovery have become more careless than before. It was not true conversion; and had they died they would have been lost. There is little hope of salvation in sickness. But such a season may never come. You may die without a moment's warning. Though in health today, you may be dead tomorrow. And are you, when life is so uncertain, putting off salvation?

A prisoner is under sentence of death. He doesn't know the fatal hour, but is told, that if before it strikes he petitions the governor, his life will be spared. He says, "I'll send tomorrow." And when tomorrow comes again, "Oh, there's time enough yet; I'll wait a little longer." Suddenly his door opens, and--behold the sheriff and the executor! "Oh, wait, and I'll write the petition.' "No," they say, "the clock has struck--its too late--you must die."

Poor sinner, you are condemned. You know not when you may die. It may be this very day. You put off repentance till tomorrow; but tomorrow you may be in hell. Christ knocks today; but remember death may knock tomorrow. Though you keep your best Friend outside, death will burst in, and hurry you away to the judge. Come to Jesus today. He is willing to save today. Heaven's gate is open today. Tomorrow may be too late.

Matthew 24:36-51 "But concerning that day and hour no one knows, not even the angels of heaven, nor the Son, but the Father only.

For as were the days of Noah, so will be the coming of the Son of Man. For as in those days before the flood they were eating and drinking, marrying and giving in marriage, until the day when Noah entered the ark, and they were unaware until the flood came and swept them all away, so will be the coming of the Son of Man. Then two men will be in the field; one will be taken and one left. Two women will be grinding at the mill; one will be taken and one left. Therefore, stay awake, for you do not know on what day your Lord is coming. But know this, that if the master of the house had known in what part of the night the thief was coming, he would have stayed awake and would not have let his house be broken into. Therefore you also must be ready, for the Son of Man is coming at an hour you do not expect.

"Who then is the faithful and wise servant, whom his master has set over his household, to give them their food at the proper time? Blessed is that servant whom his master will find so doing when he comes. Truly, I say to you, he will set him over all his possessions. But if that wicked servant says to himself, 'My master is delayed,' and begins to beat his fellow servants and eats and drinks with drunkards, the master of that servant will come on a day when he does not expect him and at an hour he does not know and will cut him in pieces and put him with the hypocrites. In that place there will be weeping and gnashing of teeth.

Matthew 25:1-13 "Then the kingdom of heaven will be like ten virgins who took their lamps and went to meet the bridegroom. Five of them were foolish, and five were wise. For when the foolish took their lamps, they took no oil with them, but the wise took flasks of oil with their lamps. As the bridegroom was delayed, they all became drowsy and slept. But at midnight there was a cry, 'Here is the bridegroom! Come out to meet him.' Then all those virgins rose and trimmed their lamps. And the foolish said to the wise, 'Give us some of your oil, for our lamps are going out.' But the wise answered, saying, 'Since there will not be enough for us and for you, go rather to the dealers and buy for yourselves.' And while they were going to buy, the bridegroom came, and those who were ready went in with him to the marriage feast, and the door was shut. Afterward the other virgins came also, saying, 'Lord, lord, open to us.' But he answered, 'Truly, I say to you, I do not know you.' Watch therefore, for you know neither the day nor the hour.

Luke 12:16-21 And he told them a parable, saying, "The land of a rich man produced plentifully, and he thought to himself, 'What shall I do, for I have nowhere to store my crops?' And he said, 'I will do this: I will tear down my barns and build larger ones, and there I will store all my grain and my goods. And I will say to my soul, "Soul, you have ample goods laid up for many years; relax, eat, drink, be merry."' But God said to him, 'Fool! This night your soul is required of you, and the things you have prepared, whose will they be?' So is the one who lays up treasure for himself and is not rich toward God."

Luke 13:24-28 "Strive to enter through the narrow door. For many, I tell you, will seek to enter and will not be able.

When once the master of the house has risen and shut the door, and you begin to stand outside and to knock at the door, saying, 'Lord, open to us,' then he will answer you, 'I do not know where you come from.' Then you will begin to say, 'We ate and drank in your presence, and you taught in our streets.' But he will say, 'I tell you, I do not know where you come from. Depart from me, all you workers of evil!' In that place there will be weeping and gnashing of teeth, when you see

Abraham and Isaac and Jacob and all the prophets in the kingdom of God but you yourselves cast out.

Acts 24:25 And as he reasoned about righteousness and self-control and the coming judgment, Felix was alarmed and said, "Go away for the present. When I get an opportunity I will summon you."

2 Corinthians 6:1-2 Working together with him, then, we appeal to you not to receive the grace of God in vain. For he says, "In a favorable time I listened to you, and in a day of salvation I have helped you." Behold, now is the favorable time; behold, now is the day of salvation.

Hebrews 3:7-11 Therefore, as the Holy Spirit says, "Today, if you hear his voice, do not harden your hearts as in the rebellion, on the day of testing in the wilderness, where your fathers put me to the test and saw my works for forty years. Therefore I was provoked with that generation, and said, 'They always go astray in their heart; they have not known my ways.' As I swore in my wrath, 'They shall not enter my rest.'"

Chapter 31

YOU MUST PERISH IF YOU DO NOT COME

"What must I do to be saved?" "Believe in the Lord Jesus Christ." "What must I do to be lost?" "Neglect the available salvation." It is not necessary to do anything. We are lost already. Jesus offers to save us; but if we reject his offer, we remain as we are. If a man were bitten by a deadly serpent, but refused to apply the only remedy, he must die. The gospel is the only cure for the soul; and if we neglect it, sin kills us. You need not be a thief or a murderer to lose your soul. You may conform to all the outward ordinances of religion, but if you do not come to Jesus, you are lost. Consider the solemn words, "How shall we escape, if we NEGLECT so great a salvation?" Escape is impossible, if we neglect the only means of safety.

A boat is drawn by the current of the river near to the foaming cataract, where it must perish; but there is one solitary projecting rock near which it passes, where some men are waiting with a rope. Suppose the crew neglect to catch it--how can they escape? Neglect is their ruin. Jesus alone can save the soul. " And there is salvation in no one else, for there is no other name under heaven given among men by which we must be saved."

Oh, sinner, your damnation is sure, if you reject Jesus. And how great will be your guilt and punishment! There remains no more sacrifice for sin. How much punishment, do you think, will be deserved by the one who has trampled underfoot the Son of God, and has profaned the blood of the covenant by which he was sanctified, and has outraged the Spirit of grace?"

What delusion has seized you? Do you think God will not execute his threatenings, that you will escape his piercing eye, or the rocks will cover you? Vain hopes. There is no escape except by coming to Jesus, and simple neglect is certain perdition. "Because I called, but you refused, I also will laugh at your calamity, I will mock when your fear comes. Then shall they call, but I will not answer; they shall seek me, but shall not find me; for they did not chose the fear of the Lord, and despised all my reproof."

O sinner, escape this awful threatening. Jesus now stands with open arms. He entreats you to come and be saved. Refuse his grace no longer. Come with all your sins and sorrows--come just as you are--come at once. He will in no way cast you out. Come to Jesus. Come to Jesus.

Proverbs 1:24-31 Because I have called and you refused to listen, have stretched out my hand and no one has heeded, because you have ignored all my counsel and would have none of my reproof, I also will laugh at your calamity; I will mock when terror strikes you, when terror strikes you like a storm and your calamity comes like a whirlwind, when distress and anguish come upon you. Then they will call upon me, but I will not answer; they will seek me diligently but will not find me. Because they hated knowledge and did not choose the fear of the LORD, would have none of my counsel and despised all my reproof, therefore they shall eat the fruit of their way, and have their fill of their own devices.

John 3:14-21 And as Moses lifted up the serpent in the wilderness, so must the Son of Man be lifted up, that whoever believes in him may have eternal life.

"For God so loved the world, that he gave his only Son, that whoever believes in him should not perish but have eternal life. For God did not send his Son into the world to condemn the world, but in order that the world might be saved through him.

Whoever believes in him is not condemned, but whoever does not believe is condemned already, because he has not believed in the name of the only Son of God. And this is the judgment: the light has come into the world, and people loved the darkness rather than the light because their works were evil. For everyone who does wicked things hates the light and does not come to the light, lest his works should be exposed. But whoever does what is true comes to the light, so that it may be clearly seen that his works have been carried out in God."

John 3:36 Whoever believes in the Son has eternal life; whoever does not obey the Son shall not see life, but the wrath of God remains on him.

Acts 4:12 And there is salvation in no one else, for there is no other name under heaven given among men by which we must be saved."

Hebrews 2:1-3 Therefore we must pay much closer attention to what we have heard, lest we drift away from it. For since the message declared by angels proved to be reliable, and every transgression or disobedience received a just retribution, how shall we escape if we neglect such a great salvation? It was declared at first by the Lord, and it was attested to us by those who heard,

Hebrews 10:26-31 For if we go on sinning deliberately after receiving the knowledge of the truth, there no longer remains a sacrifice for sins, but a fearful expectation of judgment, and a fury of fire that will consume the adversaries. Anyone who has set aside the law of Moses dies without mercy on the evidence of two or three witnesses. How much worse punishment, do you think, will be deserved by the one who has trampled underfoot the Son of God, and has profaned the blood of the covenant by which he was sanctified, and has outraged the Spirit of grace? For we know him who said, "Vengeance is mine; I will repay." And again, "The Lord will judge his people." It is a fearful thing to fall into the hands of the living God.

I will make the decision

I WILL COME TO JESUS--

Just as I am, without one plea But that thy blood was shed for me, And that thou bidst me come to thee, O Lamb of God, I come!

Just as I am, and waiting not, To rid my soul of one dark blot, To thee whose blood can cleanse each spot, O Lamb of God, I come!

Just as I am—poor, wretched blind— Sight, riches, healing of the mind, Yes, all I need, in thee to find, O Lamb of God, I come!

Just as I am—though tossed about, With many a conflict, many a doubt, With fears within, and foes without, O lamb of God, I come!

Words by Charlotte Elliott

Printed in Great Britain
by Amazon

56734516R00096